Untapped Agility

UNTAPPED AGILITY

SEVEN LEADERSHIP MOVES TO

TAKE YOUR TRANSFORMATION

TO THE NEXT LEVEL

JESSE FEWELL

BK
Berrett–Koehler Publishers, Inc.

3 9082 14115 6904

Berrett-Koehler Publishers, Inc.
1333 Broadway, Suite 1000
Oakland, CA 94612-1921
Tel: (510) 817-2277   Fax: (510) 817-2278   www.bkconnection.com

Ordering Information
Quantity sales. Special discounts are available on quantity purchases by corporations, associations, and others. For details, contact the "Special Sales Department" at the Berrett-Koehler address above.
Individual sales. Berrett-Koehler publications are available through most bookstores. They can also be ordered directly from Berrett-Koehler: Tel: (800) 929-2929; Fax: (802) 864-7626; www.bkconnection.com.
Orders for college textbook / course adoption use. Please contact Berrett-Koehler: Tel: (800) 929-2929; Fax: (802) 864-7626.

Distributed to the U.S. trade and internationally by Penguin Random House Publisher Services.

Berrett-Koehler and the BK logo are registered trademarks of Berrett-Koehler Publishers, Inc.

Printed in the United States of America

Berrett-Koehler books are printed on long-lasting acid-free paper. When it is available, we choose paper that has been manufactured by environmentally responsible processes. These may include using trees grown in sustainable forests, incorporating recycled paper, minimizing chlorine in bleaching, or recycling the energy produced at the paper mill.

Library of Congress Cataloging-in-Publication Data

Names: Fewell, Jesse, author.
Title: Untapped agility : seven leadership moves to take your transformation to the next level / by Jesse Fewell.
Description: Oakland, CA : Berrett-Koehler Publishers, [2020] | Includes bibliographical references and index.
Identifiers: LCCN 2020002021 | ISBN 9781523088300 (paperback ; alk. paper) | ISBN 9781523088317 (pdf) | ISBN 9781523088324 (epub)
Subjects: LCSH: Organizational change—Management. | Leadership.
Classification: LCC HD58.8 .F48 2020 | DDC 658.4/092—dc23
LC record available at https://lccn.loc.gov/2020002021

First Edition
26 25 24 23 22 21 20   10 9 8 7 6 5 4 3 2 1

Book producer: Westchester Publishing Services
Text designer: Westchester Publishing Services
Cover designer: Adam Johnson

To all the change makers out there,
and to Seema, who's changed me the most

Contents

Foreword

Luke Hohmann, author of *Innovation Games*

It turns out that computers can teach us something about transformational leadership.

When you run a software program, usually something happens. That's kind of the point of a program, right? You click a button or you type in a command, and instantly you see some sort of feedback. You run the program, it executes, and then it's done. In other words, it comes to a halt.

But this isn't always the case. Sometimes a program runs for a really long time. Sometimes even for an infinitely long amount of time. This creates a problem: there's no way to actually tell whether a program will ever be done. In fact, it's one of the most fundamental problems in computer science, so fundamental that solving it changed both mathematics and computer science forever.

Let's imagine a program like this:

```
while(true) {
   print("I am running.")
}
```

Since "true" will always be true, we can see that this program will be printing for a very long time. It will never halt. This is a pretty simple example, but what about more complex programs like gene sequencing, data mining, or stock predictions? The question is known as the *halting problem*.

An obvious solution is to run the program and see what happens. If it runs and then stops, the problem is solved. But wait, some programs take a very long time to finish. What if our program didn't halt now but will halt after, say, one hour, or one day, or one thousand years? How do we know if we should terminate the run or keep going? That's the challenge: unless you run the program, you don't know if it halts. And even if you run it, you won't know if it halts unless you wait potentially forever.

The brilliant mathematician Alan Turing, considered by many to be the father of computer science, proved that it is impossible to tell if an arbitrary program will halt once it starts running. And when I say impossible, I don't just mean hard. I mean literally, mathematically impossible. So the only response is to work around the problem: watch and adapt. We can monitor and limit the expected resources the program will consume (time, memory, or CPU processing) and stop the program if any of these resources are exceeded. Once stopped, we can examine, adjust, and try again.

Agile transformations often experience the organizational equivalent of the halting problem. We don't know how long it will take. We don't know if the transformation will make things better. We don't exactly know what the organization will look like when we're finished. Most leaders will argue they have a fiduciary responsibility to have answers to these questions before going any further.

Unfortunately, Turing showed us we do not get to have the luxury of those answers; we cannot know whether or where the transformation will end. Instead, the only way to know if a transformation will be successful is to start it, monitor its resource consumption, and then adjust as needed to keep things on track.

In this marvelous contribution to the agile canon, my friend and colleague Jesse Fewell shares powerful advice on how to start, monitor, and yes, if necessary, pivot your agile transformation to success.

Untapped Agility

CHAPTER 1

Transformation Frustration

Expectations were like fine pottery. The harder you held them, the more likely they were to crack.
—*Brandon Sanderson, The Way of Kings*

This book is about leading change, and we need to start with a story. I once worked for a startup entrepreneur named Jeff who told me a business story so compelling, I will never forget it.

Jeff was a colorful character, whose first career was that of a restaurateur. Jeff was a force of nature and over the years worked his way up from busboy to server to sommelier to general manager to restaurant builder. One year, he was sent off to a hot new location to build the latest Planet Hollywood, the franchise eateries famous for their décor patterned after the movies. Their playbook was solid, with key criteria for geography, layout, furniture, décor. These guys knew how to build a repeatable premier experience. The boss told him, "Your new location build-out is a slam dunk. The space is in a great location, and we got the old building at a steal. Just renovate and launch, and this place will make money."

With his orders in hand, Jeff traveled to the property to meet the contractors who would construct the new location. When he arrived, he saw firsthand the easy access from the main roads and the busy retail foot traffic. Everything looked promising. Until he went inside.

1

There, standing in the middle of his promising new restaurant space, was a giant, ugly column. It was a massive monstrosity; it took several people holding hands to surround it.

Jeff summoned his new team and said, "Hi there. Nice to meet you all. I'm hoping someone can tell me, what is *that*?" "Well, boss, *that* is a load-bearing column. We can't demolish it, so we'll have to build around it." Frustration welling up inside him, Jeff said, "That thing consumes dining space and is a giant eyesore. What do we do?" Immediately the team started brainstorming:

Could they use it as a bar? Nope, too centrally located inside the dining space.

Could they use it as the guest reception desk? Nope, it was too big to do that elegantly.

Could they move the point-of-sale systems there? Nope, too far from some of the dining sections.

The team was stumped. In all his years of expertise, Jeff had never come across anything like this. Eventually they realized the column could serve no functional purpose. It was just there. Jeff asked the team, "What if we just let it be? We could at least make it appealing and hang décor items on it." "Maybe," said one of the contractors. "But the prop mounts are designed for flat walls, not curved surfaces." Another chimed in, "Instead of hammers, we could use paint. How about a custom mural depicting various movie scenes?" The group got a little more animated, and another person wondered, "What if that mural rotated slowly around that column, so that customers got to see different parts of it as they dined?"

There were no silver bullets, but with some ideas in hand, they began working. After a few months of feverish scrambling, the restaurant was set to open on schedule. Meanwhile, Jeff was still nervous. Yes, the team put in their best creative efforts, but this was still very different from the standard blueprints, the standard designs, the standard brand layout. There was a ton at stake, and it just felt *wrong*.

Except customers loved it.

"This is so cool," they said. "We've never seen anything like this," they said. "We've been to Planet Hollywood locations around the world and this is our new favorite," they said. Despite the roller-coaster ride, it became Jeff's most successful project to date.

That is what untapped agility is all about.

We boost forward with a solid plan. Eventually we hit a frustrating barrier. Finally, we take the risk of rebounding on an alternate path forward.

In the world of work, fewer endeavors draw more hype and yield more frustration than the lofty goal of "business transformation." Companies around the world are facing new and unexpected challenges. More disruption, more change, more competition than ever before. For most of us, the strategic response is to reboot the organization to achieve a greater degree of agility. That almost always takes the shape of a formal change initiative to embrace one or more of those latest management buzzwords like Design Thinking, DevOps, Lean Startup, Holacracy, Scrum, or Kanban.

Unfortunately, every single one of those transformations go through the same roller-coaster ride that Jeff went through. This book is about how to ride that roller coaster without losing your mind in the process.

The Pattern of Untapped Agility

I have examined dozens of case studies and interviewed several transformation leaders to find out how they achieve the results that everyone else is finding so hard to achieve. In my research

I found a surprising pattern. Over and over, leaders walked through a familiar sequence:

1. **The Boost.** Most leaders start with a proven first step to generate momentum. They begin with "the right things." Planet Hollywood's playbook had worked before and even generated a win—the great location for the Jeff's restaurant. Moreover, Jeff and his team had good reason to turn to standard solutions: he was super successful at solving problems with that expertise. Similarly, when launching an effort to create the modern organization, conventional wisdom is a good place to start. Leaders are justified when starting with proven steps like taking initiative, mobilizing their teams, and installing best practices.

2. **The Barrier.** However, after that initial momentum, leaders encounter common human barriers. Jeff and his team struggled with the column problem because they were relying on what had worked before: practical, functional, "tidy" solutions. That column didn't play fair, and neither does change. The reason for transformation headaches is that organizations are a complex mesh of people, and the people business is a sticky business. It's not a matter of good or bad, it's a matter of reality. Once we accept the barrier, we can move forward.

3. **The Rebound.** The way forward is a different direction. Instead of merely brute-forcing the initial strategy

The Untapped Agility Pattern

through the barrier, leaders yield further gains by leaning against the concept of the original boost. Jeff's original successes were based on following established career patterns and a proven construction playbook. But that load-bearing column would not permit progress using any known established practice. The way forward needed to break the mold. So the team leaned into the awkwardness and tried a strategy that was decidedly *not* following the playbook. Many change champions will either push harder in the face of barriers or simply give up and blame everyone else. Others are able to step sideways toward breakthrough results, by using specific leadership moves.

No, your transformation is not a failure. It turns out the buy-in, the talent, the alignment, and the growth you need to break through are already in front of you; it's all simply hidden under the surface. Undiscovered. Unutilized. Untapped.

Let's take a look at how this pattern plays out on an industrial scale.

Transformations Boost Results

The good news is, these modern ways of working actually do work. Over and over again, we see data and case studies that paint a compelling picture of achieving greater outcomes through specific change initiatives. Let's take a look at the most popular modern transformation movements.

Lean Startup Has Executive Attention

The Lean Startup technique began as a way to help small ventures get aligned with their customers as quickly as possible, before running out of cash. Popularized by Eric Ries and Steve

Blank, the fundamental idea is to avoid wasting time and money on the wrong business idea. Senior leaders from Alaska Airlines to 3M saw real opportunity for applying this entrepreneurial framework to larger companies.

According to research published in the *Harvard Business Review*,[1] a meaningful percentage of corporate executives have seen the technique enable decisions based on evidence rather than instincts (67 percent), faster development of ideas (61 percent), better customer feedback (55 percent), speaking directly to customers (54 percent), and more flexibility adapting ideas through the life cycle (48 percent). Moreover, in his book *The Startup Way*,[2] Ries tells a provocative story of how the adoption of Lean Startup at General Electric accelerated good products and killed bad ones.

Agile Benefits Are Practically Guaranteed

In 2001, a small group of technology thought leaders issued an online charter known as the Manifesto for Agile Software Development.[3] It was a bold, simple statement that prioritizes customer satisfaction, frequent delivery, and empowered teamwork. In the years since, what started as a modest technology movement has exploded into a management revolution. By defining a set of core values and principles, those early advocates inspired a whole host of techniques and methodologies. But are those values, principles, and techniques actually helpful or merely hype?

Every year, the community asks themselves that very question. The most recent State of Agile Report shows a shocking result.[4] For eleven key outcomes, teams are literally more likely to get a given benefit than they are to even want it. For example:

- 43 percent want agile for more quality, but 47 percent got it.
- 51 percent wanted more productivity, but a full 61 percent got it.

- 62 percent were motivated by more adaptability, yet 69 percent achieved it.

For eleven key outcomes, teams are literally more likely to get a given benefit than they are to even want it.

Put another way, if you set out to improve your adaptability, productivity, customer alignment, predictability, quality, visibility, morale, risk, engineering discipline, or remote collaboration, then it is a statistical slam dunk you'll get those things. Meanwhile, the Agile Alliance has amassed a database of nearly 200 experience reports describing in more detail how agile methods have improved work around the world.[5] Indeed, a Google search for "agile case studies" yields over 34 million hits.

Suffice it to say, agile works. There's evidence to support it. And people know it.

DevOps Is a Big Boost to the Bottom Line

As popular as agile became in the tech industry, one group in particular felt left out: operations and infrastructure. In 2009, a number of those professionals convened their own mini-conference, discussing how to automate traditionally manual operations tasks, how to build technology that was "operations-proof," and how to bridge the organizational silos between those who build software and those who support it. Those concepts were posted on social media, tagged with #DevOps, and promptly went viral.[6] It sparked a new conversation about expanding agility to include both R&D and operations. A decade later, DevOps has evolved into its own movement with a vibrant $3.5 billion market.[7]

And there's good reason. In a seminal 2014 research white paper,[8] we see two compelling discoveries:

- "Strong IT performance is a competitive advantage. Firms with high-performing IT organizations were twice as likely to exceed their profitability, market share and productivity goals."
- "DevOps practices improve IT performance. IT performance strongly correlates with well-known DevOps practices such as use of version control and continuous delivery. The longer an organization has implemented— and continues to improve upon—DevOps practices, the better it performs. And better IT performance correlates to higher performance for the entire organization."

So, DevOps is much more than a mechanical upgrade of the technology infrastructure used by those Ops people. It correlates to the kind of organizational performance that doubles your chances of business success.

Lean Startup, Agile, and DevOps are just three of the several methods associated with agility, but already you can see the case is closed. These transformations work. Over time, doing things differently yields better results. We're done, right? We won, didn't we?

And Yet, Everyone Is Frustrated

Despite all those benefits, the picture is not all rainbows and unicorns. On the one hand, we have thousands of organizations declaring victory with transforming business using these modern movements. On the other hand, a lot of people are very, very frustrated.

Our Staff Are Disgruntled

Change is hard. Just ask the people trying to make it happen. In a 2017 change management study,[9] 60 percent of those championing agile ways of working experienced "moderately to very severe resistance." Consider for a moment: that means staff resist concepts intended to empower them, managers resist changes proven to improve productivity and predictability, and executives resist transformations shown to boost the bottom line. That is more than ironic, it's deeply discouraging.

Even more concerning, those leaders who are declaring transformational victory are not supported by their staff. The 2018 State of DevOps reports a serious perception gap around the maturity of modern organizational capabilities.[10] Specifically, an average 58 percent of executives believe they've achieved a given practice, while only 37 percent of the teams on the ground see it that way. This means a significant number of those working on the ground have the unhappy situation of hearing their boss say, "Oh, we're agile now," when from their perspective, it's just not true.

Thought Leaders See Their Vision Perverted

Meanwhile, some of the very people who started these movements are rather perturbed. The more popular agility becomes, the more large corporations want to jump on board. Eventually we start to see some common *Dilbert*-esque patterns showing up: proprietary methodologies, expensive tools and templates, glitzy conferences, and bloated certifications.

In a viral, blistering blog post,[11] one of the creators of that original Agile Manifesto, Dave Thomas, declared the whole thing to be dead, saying, "The word 'agile' has been subverted to the point where it is effectively meaningless, and what passes for an agile community seems to be largely an arena for consultants and vendors to hawk services and products."

"The word 'agile' has been subverted to the point where it is effectively meaningless, and what passes for an agile community seems to be largely an arena for consultants and vendors to hawk services and products." — Dave Thomas

---

Indeed, pioneer of the Lean Startup movement Steve Blank recently pondered his own impending irrelevance.[12] His movement was born of the great recession, when startup capital was scarce. Now, with so many startup companies going IPO, institutional investors are throwing much more money at ventures than ever before. Naturally, this invites some executives to scoff at the notion of empirically measuring and iterating on small bets. "How quaint. That's, like, so five years ago."

Granted, Blank is willing to let bazillionaires blow their funds prematurely, but he and others are growing annoyed that other mainstream organizations are whittling away the discipline and rigor they were initially able to inspire.[13]

As these pioneers see it, traditional business practices are more successful at diluting agility, rather than the original vision of agility transforming business practices. Although always a concern since day one, this sentiment has only been getting louder in recent years.[14]

The true believers feel betrayed.

Executives Are Still Deeply Worried

Today, General Electric is not what we thought it should be. In less than a year after Ries published their Lean Startup case study,

GE suffered several layoffs, divested some of its oldest business units, and was removed from the Dow Jones industrial average. Of course, public struggles invite critics, who argue that the Lean Startup method was at best ineffective and at worst instrumental in those struggles. The agile community quickly shot back. Ries's colleague Steve Blank drafted a strong rebuttal defending the method, saying, "No innovation program, lean or otherwise, would have helped the dismal performance of its power segment."[15] That is poor consolation to executives who are now faced with a dilemma: either agile methods don't work at all, or they simply won't work well enough to save their dying organization.

They're not the only ones. I was personally involved at an agile transformation at Xerox in 2018, and despite the well-intentioned efforts of very intelligent people, layoffs continued as part of an ongoing restructuring of the company. For some organizations, these transformations may well be too little too late. As a result, senior leaders are worried whether these techniques will work for them. A recent study involving over 1,000 organizational executives found only 47 percent believe they can extract sustainable value from agile transformations.[16] Indeed, only half (51 percent) believe they can generate even short-term wins, let alone the long-term impact.

Despite the success some leaders are seeing, there is still a crisis of transformation confidence among many C-suites.

The Barriers

On the one hand, we see almost guaranteed benefits, improved bottom lines, and a corpus of successful case studies. On the other hand, we see a broad set of leaders, practitioners, and innovators declaring "agile has failed our expectations." It begs the question: why? Why on earth is my transformation not performing? Why am I not seeing the results I hoped for? Why is my boss so agitated? Why have we been let down by agile, Design Thinking, Lean Startup, DevOps, and all the other variations of modern management?

These questions have been asked many times. I've collected and compared several industry surveys from 2017 to 2019 that describe the state of modern practices around the world. If you add it up, it's nearly 6,500 people across industries, across all kinds of sectors, all telling the same story as to what barriers are impeding the full potential of their transformation.[17]

Here's what people are consistently saying is holding us back:

- **Culture and structure (nine mentions in four surveys).** Whether it's "minimal collaboration and knowledge sharing" or "shifting from a command-and-control culture" or "lack of trust" universally, leaders and staff alike have observed the organization itself is its biggest barrier to change.
- **Insufficient resources (six mentions in five surveys).** From "insufficient training and education" to lacking the "necessary people or funding," people feel critical elements to success are missing.
- **Inconsistent and complex processes (seven mentions in three surveys).** Another key obstacle to improvement is just how complicated companies are internally. Staffs feel overwhelmed by "lack of standardized mechanisms," a "jumble of legacy processes," and even inconsistent terminology.
- **General resistance to change (four mentions in three surveys).** Meanwhile, there's inertia. Given the "pervasiveness of traditional development methods" and the general difficulty of "behavior change," it makes sense that you'll often hear, "But this is how we've always done things."

- **Existing roles and responsibilities (five mentions in two surveys).** People like knowing where they stand. You may not be surprised to hear these transformations have project managers and project management offices feeling very much in limbo. But senior leaders also worry that these empirical, customer-driven approaches "threaten executives' decision-making authority."
- **Business context (six mentions in three surveys).** No two organizations are the same. Therefore, the unique dynamics of your business can seem fundamentally incompatible with faster delivery, collaboration, or transparency. It could be really hard to handle "regulatory compliance," or "increased [product] complexity," or "to create a [prototype] in our industry."
- **Inadequate leadership support (four mentions in four surveys).** We hear over and over again the need to "get leadership buy-in" for working a better way. Despite the fact that most transformations are launched by executives, staff still does not feel supported.

Wow. There it is. These are the reasons we aren't as agile/lean/digital/innovative as we expected we would be by now. Now that we got that off our chests, it's time for a reality check. These are all legitimate concerns, but I have a rude awakening for everyone: these challenges will never go away. The barriers will always be there. Therefore, we have to learn how to deal with them.

These challenges will never go away. The barriers will always be there. Therefore, we have to learn how to deal with them.

The Rebound

The Planet Hollywood playbook kickstarted Jeff's project. But that playbook only got him so far. He didn't do anything wrong, he simply took his boost to the inevitable crossroads. That barrier forced him to explore doing something that was decidedly not in the playbook.

Marcus Aurelius wrote: "Our actions may be impeded, but there can be no impeding our intentions or dispositions. Because we can accommodate and adapt. The mind adapts and converts to its own purposes the obstacle to our acting. The impediment to action advances action. What stands in the way becomes the way." Just like the giant column in Jeff's restaurant, the thing that hinders us the most is the very thing we need to address. Put

The Seven Leadership Moves

Stop selling, start aligning
• Generate buy-in with the big picture and personal desire

Give it away
• Enlist other champions despite the changes they make

Throw the textbook away
• Find your way by breaking free from textbook techniques

Master "no"
• Achieve focus by ruthlessly deferring projects and improvements

Attack culture and structure together
• Shepherd the intangible through tangible experiments

Look in the mirror
• Enable their transformation by mastering your own

Own the narrative
• Build confidence and credibility by reframing failure as progress

another way, the obstacle he faced and the ones we just listed quite literally *are* the job of transformation.

I know, I know—that may be a great sound bite, but it's not a solution. What do we do?

In this book, I detail seven leadership moves to rebound into untapped agility. The rebound is about (1) understanding the side effects of our initial strategy, and then (2) moving with intent toward the seemingly opposite approach. It's important to note that the rebound is not about undoing the momentum generated. Rather, it's about leveraging the other side of the proverbial coin, the yin to the yang.

The figure shows those seven leadership moves. This is just a teaser. We will dedicate a chapter to each one.

Three Leadership Personas

To help us understand how these patterns and moves apply to all leaders of all walks, we will be using three personas. Ted, Maria, and Emmit encapsulate the varying expectations and struggles experienced by leaders at different levels in the organization. These three personas will help humanize the issues at hand. We'll be able to see the transformation journey through their eyes, and thus make sense of it on a personal level.

These are overgeneralizations, as all personas are. The sample titles are not exclusive to any persona. You will likely see aspects of your actual role represented in each. In truth, that reflects the complexity of the challenges we face.

Defining Agility

Throughout this book, we will use the term *agility* to refer to any of the modern management methods related to the kind of empowered, collaborative, adaptive, customer-driven speed of work

The Three Leadership Personas

Ted
Team Lead

Title: Senior member of professional staff
Leadership role: Influential, role-model contributor
Age: 31

Ted carries a lot of responsibilities. He has a solid reputation as the go-to guy for most technical problems. On any given project he may be the technical lead or project coordinator, but he often gets pulled onto operational issues.
Pains: His primary pain is workload. Being involved in so many different things keeps the job interesting and makes him feel valued. However, he has little patience for the old-company busywork and bureaucracy that afflict the office.
On agility: His interest in agility is around doing things right, the modern way. He believes in the theory behind agility but has serious doubts anyone else on the team could step up to new ways of working, never mind the management that's been here forever.

Maria
Manager

Title: Senior director, new projects
Leadership role: People manager for seven direct reports
Age: 43

During her ten years with the company, Maria has held various roles. Moving from PMO manager to development director to head to innovation lead, she has helped her develop solid working relationships with her peers.
Pains: More than anything, Maria feels her department is held back from its full potential. She wants to generate results toward the current strategy but sees inefficiencies and dependencies in the other groups. She's never been a touchy-feely manager.
On agility: She's curious how agility could help her pain points, and she experimented with one or two methods in the past. But given that executives have come and gone, each with very different philosophies, she wonders when, if ever, will be the right time to make a serious push for it.

Emmit
Executive

Title: Associate vice president, strategic execution
Leadership role: Leader of leaders, responsible for four managers who collectively supervise 30 to 40 employees
Age: 51

Emmit is new to the organization, and he believes his new role carries a mandate for change. With growing competitive pressure, the job is to raise the bar on innovation, execution, and customer satisfaction. He's had success in the past doing this and is excited to get going.
Pains: The sheer volume of issues is daunting. He's still learning the organization's culture and structure. But so far, the talent gaps, the fragmented portfolio, and the mishmash of vendors all make it hard to know where to begin.
On agility: As a student of the industry, Emmit is aware of how agility has helped other companies overcome challenges similar to those facing the company.

Three Categories of Transformation Leader

Persona	Team Lead	Manager	Executive
Organization level	Influential contributor	Has direct reports	Leader of leaders
Mandate	Responsibility for work	Authority over budget and people	Accountability for organizational outcomes
Primary value	Tactical excellence	Strategic results	Visionary direction

that increases organizational performance. You may or may not be familiar with some of these methods, such as Scrum, Kanban, DevOps, Lean Startup, Design Thinking, and so forth. Don't worry about it—I'll offer a high-level explanation of these terms as they come up. Additionally, we've posted a more thorough comparison of these movements at the book website Untapped-Agility.com. That said, the specific agility method/framework/technique we discuss in a given chapter is not the point. Instead, you will see through each chapter that the key learnings are about change, and those lessons are the same regardless of which method we are using to transform.

Summary

In this chapter, we've defined the problem of "transformation frustration." In our pursuit to achieve more collaborative, innovative, competitive workplaces, we've learned:

- **There are benefits to transformation.** Regardless of which flavor of agility you choose, the data shows positive outcomes from the journey.
- **The frustrations and barriers are common.** Leaders encounter the same roadblocks over and over. They're

universal. They're recurring. They're holding us back from the true potential we know we can achieve.

- **This impacts all leaders.** The barriers impact all leaders, whether you are a tactical team lead, a strategic manager, or a visionary executive. The good news? You can leverage any and all of the seven forward moves, regardless of your title.

We all suffer the same pain. We all have access to the same gain.

Let's get started.

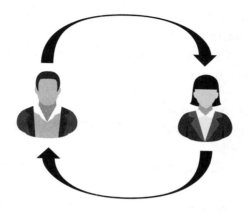

CHAPTER 2

Stop Selling, Start Aligning

Motivation will almost always beat mere talent.
—*Jason Buchanan*

G retchen was full of enthusiasm.
    In 2011, the digital arm of a global medical device manu-
facturer was slogging through business as usual. They needed a
new jolt of energy to drive more innovation out the door and
into the hands of medical providers and patients. Gretchen
Swecker was hired as the leader of the project management
office (PMO) to make that happen.

To get a head start, she attended a workshop on Scrum, a
popular innovation framework with a funny name that comes
from rugby. It describes the extreme teamwork that comes with
empowering a small team to focus on a single common goal for

a few weeks at a time, and removing anything that gets in the way of that goal.[1] Gretchen was inspired and set forth to install Scrum back at the office.

Her role allowed her to get an audience with key influencers, where she explained how changing some policies could yield a faster delivery of a stronger product. But some of her new coworkers didn't see it that way:

"This won't work for us."

"Working that fast doesn't fit regulated industries like medical devices."

"We've been doing things our way for a long time. Why change?"

"My managers are very concerned about delegating too much control to individual contributors, and I have to listen to my people."

That was the beginning of what would be a multiyear slog. Even with the group's executive leader offering his vocal public support, a number of Gretchen's peers were deeply skeptical and hesitant to jump on board. She reflects on the journey this way:

Our broader leadership team was not unified and supportive of the transformation. It was very divided at that time. I personally learned from that experience that any kind of transformation of that degree has to begin with leadership awareness and buy-in before trying to move to the teams. Otherwise, you end up with these really difficult mixed messages to the team. They're trying to do the right thing and support the initiative, but at the same time, they hear all the murmuring on the sidelines and sidebar conversations that are undermining the whole initiative. That is probably my biggest scar.[2]

The Problem of Getting Buy-In

Gretchen is not alone.

Over and over, we hear transformation champions struggle to get support for their initiatives. What's obvious to you is not only confusing to others but often represents a threat, which in turn inspires overt resistance, backstabbing, grumbling, and all other sorts of negativity. This frustration afflicts leaders at all levels, and it follows a predictable pattern:

- **The Boost.** Yes, it was good you leveraged your role to get started.
- **The Barrier.** And yet, they're not on board.
- **The Rebound.** So now, stop selling and start aligning.

The Pattern of Untapped Buy-In

Leaders Leverage Their Role

Ted	**Maria**	**Emmit**
Team Lead	Manager	Executive
"I've learned about the power of user stories to document customer needs. I'd like us to start using these techniques going forward, and I'll show you how to do them."	"Creativity is super important. We have some budget for skill growth, so I'll send everyone to a 2-day training on product innovation."	"We need to energize this organization. Thus, 80 percent of our projects should use agile products by the end of the fiscal year."

The Boost: Yes, It Was Good to Leverage Your Role

The best way to get started is to get started. No matter your title, you can exert influence with those around you. It makes sense, so you did something to get things moving.

The Barrier: And Yet, They're Not on Board

Despite your best efforts, you're still very much alone. As champions for better ways of working, more collaboration, more innovation, more alignment, we can see the urgency around the change. We explain it again and again, and yet we're not getting through.

Leaders Struggle with Buy-In

Ted Team Lead	Maria Manager	Emmit Executive
"They're pushing back on me at every turn."	"Why can't they see this way is easier?"	"This is a critical initiative, but I'm not seeing the sense of urgency."

The Rebound: So Now, Stop Selling and Start Aligning

The field of organizational change management has established a full body of literature over the last half-century. Although research continues, three descriptive models have emerged as the most commonly referenced and leveraged frameworks for describing successful change.

- Jeffrey Hiatt's ADKAR model is deeply popular among the project management community. It advocates that the first thing we do is (1) *raise awareness* of the need for change and (2) *create desire* to support the change on a personal level.[3]

- John Kotter's 8-Step Process has evolved over twenty years. Today's version encourages concurrent and continuous pursuit of several critical steps. The first one? *Create a sense of urgency* for the change.[4]
- Chip Heath and Dan Heath's book *Switch* was a 2010 *New York Times* best seller that detailed nine techniques across three categories. The first step in the category of "Motivation" is to *find the feeling*. Specifically, "Knowing something isn't enough to cause change. Make people feel something."[5]

Do you see the pattern? These leading change models all assert that successful change is launched with focused attention on motivators.

Change starts with "why." But that's not usually what we do. Our normal approach to change looks more like this:

1. Learn the modern way of doing things.
2. Install our favorite framework or technique.
3. Complain how everyone does it wrong.

I know because I've done it. We share our super-amazing strategy, and we wonder why people aren't as excited as we are.

Here's another one: A mid-manager believes more collaboration and creativity are needed. He buys a lot of training, sends his team to the workshops, where invariably one employee kicks off the day with an honest question: "Uh, nobody told me why I'm here. Can you, the training vendor, tell us what's going on?"

I've personally trained and coached thousands of professionals on modern management practices over the last ten years. I can tell you this happens all the time. Too many times, trainers go straight to the techniques, to the knowledge of what the change will entail. We explain these cool new things, and everyone's looking at us like we're from Mars. They're wondering, "Why do we need to change at all?"

It turns out that people are already equipped with their own motivations—and they're really powerful, at that. In order to generate the buy-in we're looking for, we want to pursue the motivators that are already latent inside the people around us. Before was the right time to leverage your role to mobilize your own motivations for moving forward. Now is the time to do the opposite and tap into their motivations.

In this chapter, we'll explore what it means to generate alignment.

- **Point to broader forces.** Rather than talking about short-term goals, tell the bigger story.
- **Stop explaining, start asking.** Rather than relying on the logic of doing things a better way, work to figure out what matters to the people you're influencing.
- **Stop pulling rank, start repeating the message.** Rather than relying on your positional power to carry the message, get ready to repeat yourself over and over.

Point to Broader Forces

What does Hiatt mean by "awareness of the need for change"? What does Kotter mean by "create a sense of urgency"? It means emphasizing the driver *behind* the change—the "so what?" and the "who cares?"

In one of most popular TED talks of all time,[6] Simon Sinek walks through the drivers for brand loyalty, purchasing, voting, and any kind of choice-driven behavior. In short, he asserts that

"Nobody buys what you do; they buy why you do it." His message went viral, because it just makes sense.

People don't buy thousand-dollar iPhones because of the features. They buy them for the aspirational association with a luxury technology. Similarly, the Apple Watch is galactically more expensive than the Timex I can buy at the local superstore; it's not about telling the time. Apple has become the world's largest watchmaker because people want to wear the most sophisticated upper-middle-class accessory. People don't buy Harley-Davidson motorcycles because they're the fastest or most fuel efficient. They buy them because they identify with the attitude they convey. If you want to use the carpool lanes to get to work, just buy any motorcycle. If you want to connect with your inner badass, buy a Harley.

"Nobody buys what you do; they buy why you do it."
—Simon Sinek

In fact, Harvard business professor Gerald Zaltman tells us that 95 percent of all decisions people make are subconscious.[7] That isn't to say we don't value logic. We do value the logical, quantitative substance in different choices in front of us. However, all that substance gets mushed into our brain with other cognitive forces.

Sinek also describes it this way. Have you ever been in a meeting where you explain an obvious opportunity where there's a clear ROI and the leader says, "Yeah, I get your facts and figures, but it just doesn't feel right." What do you mean it doesn't feel right? Who makes decisions based on their gut? As it turns out, 95 percent of everyone who makes a decision. Now, we do make those subconscious decisions with the influence of data, with the influence of return and reward that our rational mind bakes into the subconscious. It's there, it's just not as explicit; it's not cause and effect. It's much more nuanced.

Sinek challenges us that explaining the value of something on its own doesn't cut it. So, if that's true, then what do I tell people about my transformation? Good question. Here are three messages that are very real drivers for change in the way work gets done.

Message 1: Your Product Is Old News

Go to a leader, go to a manager, go to the tech lead, and ask them, "What are you most concerned about?" It's a future-oriented question, outside of the immediate context. At the organizational level, a lot of people might not be aware that they need to be concerned about the fact that your product is old news.

According to the U.S. Census, products are hitting adoption rates in faster and faster time frames.[8] It took more than four decades for electricity to hit critical mass. Television only took twenty-five years to achieve the same milestone. The smartphone hit 25 percent adoption in only four years. The trend is clear:

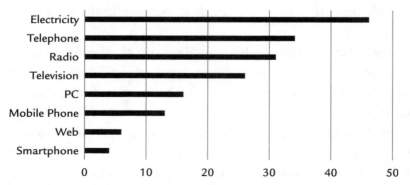

Years to Achieve Adoption by 25% of US Population

Source: 2010 U.S. Census.

products gain adoption faster than ever. As a correlation, their life spans are shorter than ever before. Just look at the world of home movies: the cathode ray tube is dead, then DVD is dead, then Blu-ray is dead.

So what we're seeing is that whatever you've done as a senior leader, department manager, product manager, or innovator, whatever you've built is about to be obsolete.

Message 2: The Workplace Has Forever Changed

I'm sure you've noticed by now that the workplace is different than it was in our parents' time. The U.K. government's Chartered Institute for Professional Development summarized these changes in their landmark Megatrends reports.[9] Here are some of the key points:

- **The workforce is older.** Since 1992, the percentage of employees aged fifty and over has increased from 21 percent to 29 percent. Meanwhile, the percentage of workers in younger age groups has decreased. From baby boomers to Generation Z, we have more age diversity in the office than ever before.
- **Workers are more educated.** In 1993, 11 percent of the working-age population had a degree. By 2011, that had shifted to 24 percent. We have more talent in the office than ever before.
- **Companies are smaller.** Since the beginning of the century, large-company jobs (250 or more people) decreased from 49 percent to 40 percent of all jobs. Meanwhile, small-company jobs (four or fewer people) increased from 11 percent to 22 percent of all jobs. We have a more decentralized economy than ever before.
- **There are more women in the office, finally.** In forty-two years, women went from 37 percent of the

workforce to 47 percent. We have more gender diversity
at the office than ever before.

This is happening not just in some industries but in every indus-
trialized country in the world. The workplace is changing.
Mr. Leader or Ms. Manager, the workforce is not interested in
working for your company as much as they used to be, unless you
adapt and respond to the dynamics in the market. For example,
many are willing to give up some of their salary so they can work
from home. Therefore, your message to managers could be like
"It might be time to transform our organization to be more com-
patible with the modern workforce reality."

Message 3: The Competition Is Out for Everyone, Including You
The competition is real. I know a lot of people who like to say,
"Well, we're government based, so we don't have competition." Oh,
really—except Amazon. Amazon's original stated mission was "to
be Earth's most customer-centric company, where customers can
find and discover anything they might want to buy online." Amazon's literal goal is to help offices bypass official procurement
and supply chains in favor of Amazon as a cheaper and faster
option.

The commercial world is even worse. Since the mid-twentieth
century, the average age of a company on the S&P 500 has shrunk
from nearly sixty years to less than twenty years.[10] Profitable companies are getting younger. In fact, between 2013 and 2017 some
very big names were pushed out of the S&P 500, including
Yahoo!, DuPont, Staples, Dun & Bradstreet, DirecTV, Dell EMC,
Bed Bath & Beyond, and Safeway.[11]

In order to compete, we need more of those organizational
capabilities we saw in chapter 1: more speed, more adaptability, more productivity, more morale, more alignment with
customers, and so on. Therefore, your pitch to an executive

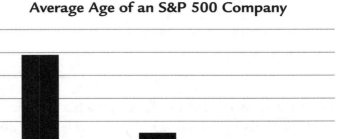

Source: Credit Suisse.

could be something like, "It might be time for our organization to transform to a more modern, competitive version of ourselves."

These three messages can align your transformation to larger, credible industry trends. This will help you connect your move to something bigger. Something real and tangible. Something more than just "because I said so."

Stop Explaining, Start Asking

It's one thing to justify a transformation at a macro scale. It's another thing to make it appealing to individuals. The way to do it is to stop selling and start aligning.

Selling is where I'm trying to get you to my perspective. It goes like this, "Maria, I believe in my bones that Lean Startup is the answer to better innovation. If you just understood what I understand, then you'd be with me. You'll be where I'm at and it will be awesome." That's selling. The problem with selling your strategy is sometimes people don't buy.

The problem with selling your strategy is sometimes people don't buy.

What if we tried something different? What if we sat down and shared thoughts? "So from your perspective, what do you see? Here's what I see from my perspective." What's in common? How can two opposing things be simultaneously true? We need to be efficient, but we also need to be innovative. Can we be both of those things? How do we do that? That dialogue requires you to ask first and tell second. Stop selling, start aligning. Selling is getting *you* to *my* perspective. Aligning is getting *us* to *our* perspective.

Approaching Team Leads

Most senior contributors just want to do good work. They're good at their jobs, and it's rewarding to take pride in the work they do every day. Whether it's writing specifications that are detailed, complete, and accurate, or building products that are

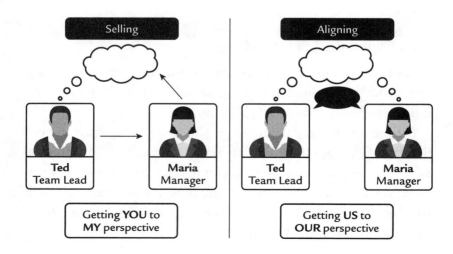

high quality with few defects, or something that's truly new and innovative and adds value, they want to do good work. They want their work to have an impact. They want to be able to see how the work they do can impact their customers and stakeholders and maybe add value for them. That's what's on their mind. Then here comes the transformation champion, ready to sell a new approach:

Selling to Ted

Ted
Team Lead

CHAMPION: I'm excited to tell you about a more collaborative way of working, where people are valued more than process.

TED: Fair enough, tell me what that means. I'm curious.

CHAMPION: Well, we use the Scrum framework to drive more collaboration. It's awesome. There are five new meetings we'll add to your schedule: backlog updates, planning meetings, daily stand-up meeting for fifteen minutes. Then, after our two-week milestone, we'll go into a half-day closeout meeting, which starts with a presentation of all of our work to managers and customers, and ends with a private lessons-learned session where your team asks challenging questions about improvements. It's all about the people. I know you'll love it.

TED: Actually, I don't think so. It sounds a lot like meetings. If that's what your version of collaboration means, I'll pass.

Here, the champion mentioned the principle of "people over process," but then spent the bulk of his breath explaining the framework. As a result, it didn't connect. What if the conversation went a little bit differently? What if you ask first about the pain points the team leader is suffering? What if *you* tell *me* how to sell to *you*?

Aligning with Ted

>   **CHAMPION:** What are your pain points these days?
>
>   **TED:** All my technical skills and the team. They're just haphazard. I'm working sixty or seventy hours because not everybody's doing the work the right way. I wish we had a higher level of talent on my team and so that's what's really worrying me these days. That's what's bothering me, that's my pain point.
>
>   **CHAMPION:** I totally understand. Hey, you know, nearly half of all agile practitioners report increased engineering discipline. That means you've got a heads or tails shot if we try some of these techniques that other people use.
>
>   **TED:** Interesting. I've tried a lot of things, and I'm willing to try some other things in order to improve discipline and excellence and skill sets. Tell me more.

Now you have an invitation to explain one or two new techniques. I recommend you don't avalanche them with all the possible practices or DevOps tool sets. Instead, you say, "Here's two or three things that I think might help." And then, boom, you've got a shared understanding. You're coming to alignment.

Approaching Managers

As transformation champions, we've got this vision about building high-performance organizations and wonderful places to work. And then we've got to deal with people in authority: program managers, PMO managers, department managers, and project managers. Given that they are the curators of the current organization, how could we ever bring them on board?

Well, it turns out they're actually people, and these people tend to be in the positions they're in because they're very results oriented. These are leaders who've gotten ahead in their careers by getting results, by coordinating people toward a goal and getting it done. So what's generally on their minds is: "I want those results, and I want a good track record of how we've been able to do it." Often they're less interested in the details and expect the talent—team leads and senior contributors—to get the job done. But they are very, very passionate about making sure the *right* things get done. Here comes our transformation champion again.

Selling to Maria

CHAMPION: I'm super excited about customer collaboration.

MARIA: Oh, that's interesting. Tell me more.

CHAMPION: It means that all your people are going to go into integrated teams called pods. They'll be cross-functional and totally empowered. They're going to have a customer representative, a product owner giving day-to-day direction to the team.

MARIA: But I do all those things today. What happens to my role?

CHAMPION: You'll still be the people manager doing annual HR responsibilities. But fundamentally, your job is to stay out of the way.

What do you think she's going to say? Will she like letting go of having input and influence on the work the team does? Not so much. What if we ask Maria questions instead: What are your pain points? What worries you? What would motivate you to make any kind of change at all?

Aligning with Maria

CHAMPION: What are your pain points?

MARIA: Well, that customer collaboration thing is a problem. I've got angry stakeholders. No matter what we do, they're disappointed, frustrated. I do think they're all working with positive intent; I don't think they're intentionally malicious. I just don't know what to do. It's frustrating and discouraging.

CHAMPION: Good thing I'm here! I'm an agile champion. I happen to know that two-thirds of all agile teams report increased alignment with customers. Did you know that?

MARIA: Really? Tell me more.

CHAMPION: We could try one or two specific techniques, like having more frequent dialogue. We could ask for a partner-based approach to leading initiatives, instead of just throwing it over the fence. Much the way we have a fully allocated initiative leader, a product manager, on our side, maybe we need a fully allocated sponsor on their side. Let's start with that.

Approaching Executives

I know what you're thinking: Okay, that sounds pretty interesting. I can see there's some potential there. But you know what, it doesn't work on executives. They've already made up their minds about things and are too busy to approach.

But it turns out they are people too. I work with senior leaders a lot, and most senior leaders are interested in building a differentiating organization. They want to have a legacy that sticks, they want to have an imprint on the organization they've been given, and so there's very real pressure to drive some momentum around that.

Granted, the seniority of a title amplifies the impact of a given leader's style. A busy executive can seem more unapproachable than a busy manager, and an opinionated senior leader can feel more close-minded than a similarly vocal junior manager. But almost every person I talk to in a senior role is thinking about how to build a better organization.

With that in mind, here is how a well-intentioned buy-in conversation might go between the transformation champion and an internal executive.

Selling to Emmit

Emmit
Executive

CHAMPION: I'm agile and I'm here to help. Digital transformation is all about building culture, a culture that's resilient to change.

EMMIT: Interesting. Tell me more.

CHAMPION: Well, culture comes from the top. So we need to adjust from command and control leadership to servant leadership. That means empowering people to self-organize.

EMMIT: But don't we need more than just a vision and an empowerment mandate? How is that going to make us more adaptable as an organization?

CHAMPION: It just will.

Not pretty, is it? Catchphrases like "command and control" and "self-organized" sound great in theory but may not connect to where a given leader is thinking at the moment. So what if instead we stop explaining and we start asking?

Aligning with Emmit

    CHAMPION: What's your major pain point here? I'm a change leader, I'm here to help evolve us to a better way of working. What are the pain points we need to solve? What do we need to evolve toward?

    EMMIT: I'll tell you what we need to evolve toward—we need to be more competitive. We can innovate pretty well, but we take too long. Every one of my managers I talk to tells me that "We can't do this and we can't do that" and that they're too constrained. All they keep asking for is more headcount, more headcount, more headcount, and I'm just exhausted.

    CHAMPION: That's interesting. Did you know that you're not alone, that the number-one driver for agility and digital transformations is speed to market? Did you know that three-fourths of everyone who goes in that direction actually gets it done? Not only are you not alone, but there are some proven ways to achieve a little bit of progress on that.

    EMMIT: Really? Tell me more.

At this point, you have an invitation to recommend one or two meaningful changes. Perhaps we authorize exactly half the number of projects this year relative to the number we authorized last year and nothing else. That way, we focus all of our resources, all of our people, on getting just those done. What if that's the only change we made an organizational level? We can double our focus, and by doubling our focus, we might double our speed to market. Now, that's a good conversation.

The question of getting buy-in is not them buying into you, but you buying into them.

In each scenario—the team lead, the manager, and the executive—we want to stop selling and start aligning, stop telling and start asking, to build a shared understanding. Meet your audience where they are, don't demand them to come where you are if they're not ready. The question of getting buy-in is not them buying into you, but you buying into them. That's the key thrust of what we're talking about. Start first by asking, find an agile outcome that resonates with them, and then begin trickling in techniques that fit.

Stop Pulling Rank, Start Repeating the Message

Remember what your parents used to say? "If I've told you once, I've told you a thousand times." The explicit message was that you couldn't be bothered to communicate effectively. The onus for understanding was on the receiver of the message, not the sender. But we've always known that kind of attitude is a cop-out. The role of parent is not enough to be heard the first time, and neither is your job title at the office sufficient to get your message across. Instead, there's a simple way to be more influential.

In a joint Harvard and Northwestern study,[12] groups of middle managers were analyzed on their communications strategies. The researchers wondered how often project managers used multiple channels (email, instant messaging, text, one-on-one conversations, group meetings) to convey the same request or message. Interestingly, the researchers found "managers who are deliberately redundant as communicators move their projects forward more quickly and smoothly than those who are not." In fact, those without formal title or reporting relationships were twice as likely to use redundant communication strategies. Harvard business professor Tsedal Neeley summarized the point, "Those without power were much more strategic, much more thoughtful about greasing the wheel."

How many times have you sent off an email and been frustrated that nobody read it? Email is our primary means of organizational communication, and it is fundamentally unreliable. The secret is to follow up, follow up, follow up.

Beware of Misnamed Motivators

When you ask these questions about leader anxieties and pain points, you might get some funny answers. I've heard a few of these, and they can be very subtle.

"We Need More Consistency"

One of the more insidious motivators is the seductive appeal of consistency. When asked why we need a transformation effort, I often hear, "We had some good pilots in various departments. Now we need to standardize our processes and scale that across the organization. We need more consistency." I challenge these team leads, managers, and executives by saying, "So what I hear you saying is that you want your legacy and your imprint on the organization to be that everyone is exactly the same and we're all working like robots without creativity or individuality."

This immediately evokes the intended reaction: "No, no, no, we're really talking about repeatability, scalability, sustainability."

There we go. These are indeed high-performance organizational outcomes. The word "consistency" is sometimes misused, and it has connotations that might bring negative side effects. When you hear it, probe on that a bit more.

"We Need More Efficiency"

Another one I hear goes something like "We can innovate a little bit, but we need to be more efficient." Again, I probe more deeply by asking, "What do you mean by that? Do you mean ROI and cost cutting and headcount reduction?" Almost always, that sparks the intended defensive reaction: "No, no, we're not laying off anyone. We just want them to do better."

Aha! They're really talking about efficiency as a synonym for high performance, for technical excellence, for just good work. When leaders advocate for "efficiency," it often means they want to come into the office and see the place humming like a well-oiled machine. Many times, that is what's desired, even if it costs a little more money. The goal is less about the textbook definition of ROI as much as productivity, quality, and excellence.

"We're Not Sure Why, We Just Know We Need To"

Finally, one of my favorites is when the answer to the "why" question is a non-answer:

> **CHAMPION:** So what are your number-one pain points and what's interesting to you about this agile conversation?
>
> **MANAGER:** We're not sure yet. We've got a three-month project to find out why we need to go agile.
>
> **CHAMPION:** Okay, so then why are we having this conversation?
>
> **MANAGER:** Oh, we just know we need to.
>
> **CHAMPION:** What led you to that conclusion?
>
> **MANAGER:** Well, everyone else is doing it.

Here they're feeling the need to be relevant, to be competitive. They're hearing that there's change in the industry and that there's a more modern way of doing work—more collaboration, more iteration. They want to be a part of that instead of being left behind.

That is a much more coherent transformation driver that others can get behind. In fact, you actually can use an assessment tool to measure the maturity of your practices against industry benchmarks.[13] Ask all your teams, "How are you doing with automating your most mundane tasks?" You'll get data that says, "You're actually right about the level of maturity for your industry." That would be a successful agile story that would get some support and interest, because now you know where you are, and you have the opportunity to get ahead.

Gretchen's Second Chance

Let's go back to Gretchen, our change leader from the beginning of the chapter. Recall she wanted to install an agile method called Scrum and got a lot of pushback. Despite that, she continued to push forward. She used the reinforcement and repetition we discussed earlier, hunkering down for the long haul. Over time, Scrum was used here and there. It was slow going, with occasional but meaningful improvements. Meanwhile, the skeptical, resistant leaders gradually left the firm or shifted their roles, which in turn created space for more improvements.

Eventually, a full five years after she started, a new conversation began to emerge. There was a growing consensus that a new digital platform was needed, and to make it a viable option, the group needed to scale the few innovation practices already in place.

The change had reached an inflection point, offering a fresh new opportunity. This time, Gretchen held back from leveraging her role. She waited. Granted, she did her own research on which additional techniques could help with the next phase of evolution. But she also listened to other voices, letting the chatter grow on its own. Soon other senior executives started emphasizing the need for the new platform. Finally, in 2016, the group had the green light to launch a second, more pervasive transformation effort spanning 150 people across twenty teams. Gretchen describes her journey this way:

> When I reflect on our second transformation many years later, that transformation was so much easier. I think we had at that point a critical mass of people who appreciated the value of agile methods. They realized that to scale, we needed to adopt the next level of management framework.
>
> You can't do it alone. You've got to lift and empower other people to be evangelists for the process. Trying to do it somewhat more in isolation back during our first transformation was just a painful and troubled approach for us. By comparison, when I look across the program today, any number of program leaders, it's not to say that they don't have criticisms and ideas of ways to improve, but they are invested in the approach. So find yourself those peers and those leaders who really can evangelize to help bring life to the program.

Summary

In this chapter, we've defined the problem of buy-in. By leveraging our positional authority as leaders, we've learned:

- **They're not connected to the "why."** Change is hard, and people need a reason to go through the struggle. Issuing a mandate will only get you so far.
- **Point to the broader forces.** Industry trends may be obvious to you but are not necessarily obvious to them. Be ready to explain the bigger picture and how it relates to your situation.

- **Stop explaining, start asking.** Our motivators are not their motivators.
- **Stop pulling rank, start repeating the message.** Once you have a context that resonates with people, repeat it again and again. It's easy for us to get distracted by the daily grind, and research shows that effective leadership involves reinforcement.

To get past the lack of buy-in, stop selling and start aligning.

CHAPTER 3

Give It Away

I have observed, throughout life, that a man may do an immense deal of good, if he does not care who gets the credit for it.

—*Father Strickland, Jesuit priest, 1863*

R andy was ready to make an impact.

A large 100-year-old manufacturing company was struggling to keep pace with the market, and recent layoffs would only serve as a temporary Band-Aid. In the wake of those moves, a newly installed CIO was determined to help turn the tide. She challenged her IT group to introduce more innovation into every facet of the organization. "We need more ideas on the table, and once those ideas are validated, we need them out to market faster than ever before. This is our number one priority."

The key strategy for this initiative was to "go agile," and Randy Angiel was hired as an external consultant to facilitate some training and chartering for the first pilot. This was a famous company, and they were ready to do some serious work. Randy was amped up about the opportunity.

The day of the pilot launch started off solid. The room was filled with the full representation needed to deliver the project: project managers, product owners, designers, technology, and operations. Granted, most of them had very little exposure to agile methods. Fortunately, the engineering group had some experience and could help spur discussion about textbook techniques. Randy had spent the morning level-setting everyone on techniques like sprints, shorter delivery cycles that would cut down timelines from months to weeks. To illustrate the concepts, they played an interactive game with marshmallows and spaghetti that got everyone laughing.

The room was energized. People were engaged. Randy was in his element. The next item on the agenda was to hear from the engineering group.

And that's when it got weird.

Randy transitioned: "Lisa, I hear you've been experimenting with these techniques for a while. Perhaps you can share how you're trying them out."

Engineering manager Lisa corrected him: "Oh, we've been sprinting for well over five years. We've got an established process."

Randy was intrigued. If engineering had been using agile techniques for years, then why did the CIO mandate an agile transformation? He probed further: "Interesting. Give us some examples."

Lisa: "The engineering teams are fully autonomous, within established guardrails. They pick assignments from an ordered backlog, working in two-week cycles. We also incorporate a high degree of the automation you mentioned this morning, which has reduced defects to near zero."

Randy: "Wow, that sounds like a well-oiled machine, and a real asset to get our initiative going. How soon will the teams be mobilized to work on this pilot?"

Lisa, nonchalantly: "Two months."

Randy: "But the CIO said this was the highest priority pilot of the highest priority initiative, to keep the company alive. We are authorized to drop everything and get started."

Lisa: "Those are fair priorities, but there's a ton of setup we need to do before the teams can start working. We need to convert the project charter into a use cases document and then into a design document. We then convert that into a list of specific features and an MVP. Finally, we convert those features into a proper backlog using the given-when-then format. Only then can we use those details to estimate all the work items and build out a release timeline. Those activities take two weeks. Each."

Ugh. They had overloaded their modern practices with a lot of other rigid documentation and planning steps. Randy knew the two-month delay was not going to fly, so he tried sparking more dialogue with an idea. "What if we replace your product backlog with the project management charter, and use that as input into engineering? That would cut out three steps and get things moving faster. We get them working right away on the most obvious work items, and do all that elaboration in parallel."

Lisa was unmoved. "Oh no, we don't do that. That would involve the project management office, which we won't do, because they would undermine our autonomy. Besides, the teams don't like their format. They like it their way, and it works for them."

Remember, the project managers were in the meeting as well. The room started to get a little tense. As the facilitator, Randy decided it was best to deflect the tension by changing the topic. "Well, let's go back to those teams and sprints. I'm impressed to hear about your two-week cycles. Does that mean once we get through the two-month upstream process, you can release every two weeks as well?"

Lisa waved her hand dismissively. "Oh no. Our engineering teams hand their work over to the quality department, which manually revalidates the validation we've already done. When they've done that, they organize a group of employees to review the release and sign off. Then a security scan is performed, and *then* we can roll it out. All of those things are done by busy people, so it takes a while."

"So how often do you release new technology to the company?"

"Every six months."

"What?"

"Yep. That's how it works. That's the benefit of our agile process."

The engineering manager was quite straight-faced, but Randy was dumbfounded. On the one hand, he just surfaced a lot of improvement opportunity. On the other hand, the company was failing, despite already practicing for years the very techniques he was hired to help them adopt.

They had a ton of agile but no agility. And there was no indication their most agile leader was interested in changing that. Tragically, the evolution ended right there. A year later, Randy saw the pilot finally crawl to a finish, well after the new transformation was canceled, and another series of layoffs hit the news.

The Problem with Impact

The paradox of going it alone is that you get going, which is virtuous. But you go alone, which is limited. Here is the pattern that proactive agility champions face over and over:

- **The Boost.** Yes, you took the initiative.
- **The Barrier.** And yet, the impact is only in your silo.
- **The Rebound.** So now, give it away.

The Pattern of Untapped Impact

The Boost: Yes, You Took the Initiative

It turns out that Lisa the engineering manager had launched her own engineering transformation years ago. She was the only one who knew about modern work methods, and waiting for other leaders to come on board would take forever. So she started a mini-transformation on her teams, and they've gotten really good at it. It makes sense. She did something to get things moving.

Leaders Take Initiative

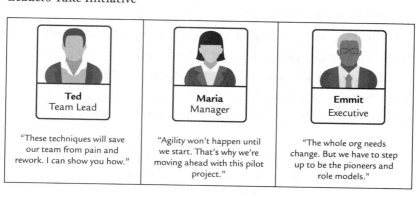

The Barrier: And Yet, the Impact Is Only in Your Silo

Despite all the growth your team has made, they're still only one part of a larger ecosystem of dependencies. You're all agile, with no agility.

Leaders Struggle with Impact

Ted Team Lead	**Maria** Manager	**Emmit** Executive
"We've improved, but now outside issues and dependencies are impacting us."	"We could do so much more, if only they would let us."	"We've done all this work, but where's the agility?"

The good news is you've built some internal competency. The bad news is you're the only champion. For the organization to achieve more, it will need that competency to scale to other leaders beyond your sphere of direct influence. Moreover, those leaders need you to show them how to do it and how to do it in their own way.

The Rebound: So Now, Give It Away

Yes, the beginning was the right time to move unilaterally. Now is the time to do the opposite—to open the change to other leaders, despite the alterations and modifications they will make to it. In this chapter, we explore the underlying problems with limited impact and how to overcome them.

- **Expectations versus reality.** Leaders have an idyllic vision in their minds, but we will discover the road to change is not paved in gold.
- **Give away your agility.** By inviting others to the table, more ideas and changes will mess with your vision, but it will expand the momentum further than you could have expected.

- **Give away your position.** Allowing your role to change will feel frightening and different, but it will solidify your legacy and your value to the organization.

Expectations versus Reality

To understand the expectation leaders have for the journey, let's use a classic software example:

Expected Transformation Journey

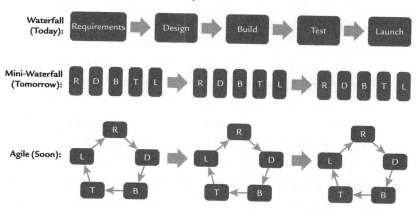

1. **First we are waterfall.** The waterfall model is a linear sequence of system development. This is the assembly line applied at scale. First we plan *all* the requirements, then we do *all* the design, then we do *all* the building, then *all* the testing, then *all* the release to operations and market. We do each project phase in sequence. You only get something when you get everything at the end. The term is a metaphor of water flowing downhill, describing how work is designed to flow downstream, one way. The metaphor emphasizes the noniterative, nonreflective nature of the sequential work cycle.

2. **Then we become mini-waterfall.** After some training
   and coaching, we're starting to transform into the
   sprints we mentioned earlier. Same life cycle, faster
   cycles, where we do *some* of the requirements, then *some*
   of the design, then *some* of the building, then *some* of
   the testing. We just did the exact same life cycle for a
   subset of the project scope. This stage is often ridiculed
   as a faulty mash-up called "Scrummerfall," because the
   firm handoffs don't look like the collaborative end state
   we want. It's not great, but it *is* progress. Rather than
   deliver the whole thing later, we deliver something
   sooner.
3. **Soon we are agile.** After more improvement, we've
   achieved nirvana. Project scope is decomposed into
   mini-deliveries, where we all work together iterating on
   those deliveries. Collaboration gurus call this "team
   swarming." We can focus on exactly one deliverable and
   do the messy teamwork that makes it bulletproof.

That's the promise. To make this happen, you just need the buy-
in from the leaders of all those departments, and we're off to the
races. But that's not how it goes.

Water-Scrum-Fall

Let's say agile catches the interest of the develop and build manager. He's intrigued by the idea of only doing one thing at a
time. So he takes initiative and begins a private agile journey.
Within weeks, his department is split into teams—Scrumming
and sprinting.

But the requirements manager is not willing to ask his staff
to break down the scope statement into smaller subsets, let alone
mini-deliveries. Her team is already overworked, and that would
be unneeded extra effort.

Water-Scrum-Fall

Moreover, the design manager is not willing to compromise on the quality of his team's design work. To generate the best possible design of the product, his team demands all the scope be considered and incorporated at once.

Finally, the test manager is okay with testing only a subset of the product at a given time. The problem is that any subsequent change may corrupt all of the previously tested items. The more often we deliver, the more often we have to retest everything we've already tested. Early delivery be damned. Agile requires rework, and rework is inefficient.

The develop and build manager has transformed, so we're no longer waterfall. But no one else has moved, so we can't be agile. Instead, we're at the intermediate limbo called "water-Scrum-fall." The result is a modernized develop-and-build department but no change in the end-to-end delivery. A whole lot of agile but no agility. And it gets worse.

The Modern Waterfall

Now that design and build manager is getting some attention. Smaller work items means progress is more trackable than before. His teams are holding public demonstrations of incomplete work; they are buzzing with activity. Then the requirements manager thinks there might be something to this. She learns about customer-oriented techniques like Lean Startup, journey maps, personas, and user stories. She challenges her team to experiment with those techniques and gets some internal momentum. Eventually, the design manager feels jealous of the cool factor he sees in the other two. He buys his team training in design techniques like Design Thinking.

The Modern Waterfall

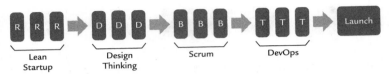

Finally, the test manager gets nervous about being the only one not on the bandwagon. She goes to an agile conference and brings back to her team several exciting new DevOps automation ideas.

All said, the transformation was leader-led, a complete success departmentally, and a complete fallacy organizationally.

And then one day the COO comes in yelling, "I just spent one million dollars on coaching and training. All of you are bragging about your transformation, and it still takes a year for us to get anything done around here. Where's all my agility? Where is it?"

This tragic story happens quite often. In 2018, Robin Dymond called this out as the "modern waterfall."[1] We have transformed every department to use modernized best practices, but by failing to work together, we've iterated our way right back to the status quo.

Give Away Your Agile

The root cause of these localized transformations is twofold. First is the frame of reference of the leaders in the organization. Most professionals will view the agile movement through the lens of their departmental function. It's natural. It's literally their job to assess reality from the perspective of what their organizational unit does. Are you a magazine layout designer? Then you will view agile from the perspective of how it relates to that.

The second root cause is perfectionism. As talented professionals, leaders like getting things right. It's how they earned their leadership roles in the first place. So when it's time to jump on the change train, we want the comfort and confidence of building excellence with the new ways of working before we involve anyone else. Involving others will distract our team's efforts to figure it out, invite unwanted suggestions and changes, and create embarrassment for our mistakes. Moreover, we learned earlier in this book that some company cultures emphasize getting it right over going fast, even for low-risk projects. That becomes a reinforcing dynamic and sustains the pattern of siloed improvement.

The asset? You took initiative to build momentum. The problem? You took initiative but didn't bring anybody with you. You didn't ask for help. Fundamentally, the degree of agility you have is determined by the degree of collaboration among your leaders, and between you and your peers.

Overcome the Dependencies

In his 1984 novel *The Goal*, management theorist Eliyahu M. Goldratt introduced the theory of constraints.[2] The theory asserts that any manageable system is limited in achieving its goals by a very small number of constraints. Any transformation should focus on finding the most limiting constraint and then reorganizing around that constraint. It's a fancy way to operationalize the concept that a chain is only as strong as its weakest link, so find the weakest link and fix it.

The theory was a pivotal elaboration on existing management theory. However, it can feel a bit ethereal and vague. Ironically, the book itself described its protagonist as consistently confused and frustrated that his management coach won't simply explain how to find the problem and fix it.

Thankfully, thought leader and consulting CEO Mike Cottmeyer translated the fancy theory into real-world transformation advice. He explains that dependencies are the problem. Dependencies are the biggest constraint in high-performing modern organizations. Moreover, these dependencies are self-inflicted wounds based on our assumptions. He explains it this way:[3]

- **Labor dependencies.** "We assume that we must optimize for individual performance and therefore we matrix team members across [multiple] projects. This creates resource dependencies between projects that did not have to exist."
- **Skill dependencies.** "We assume parts of our solution are just too complicated and must be handled by specialists. We choose to assign certain people to specific components. By default, we create dependencies between products that share the same components."
- **Knowledge dependencies.** "We assume that our product owners are too busy for the team so we assign someone else to proxy for the business. We create a dependency between the team and the business that results in a tendency to over-document and over-manage the relationship between [those asking for work and those doing the work]."

It's a compelling bit of analysis, but it leads us from one unanswered question ("What is the key constraint?") to a different unanswered question ("How do we find and resolve the dependencies?"). For that, the answer is simple: Get everyone in a room together and talk about how to deliver a given product faster than you have ever delivered anything before. Immediately, people will start to freak out. Bingo. You just found the dependencies. This practice is called big room planning and was popularized by many of the various agility methods in the industry.

If you have a collective will to invite people to the table, find the dependencies, and then transform the organization to overcome those dependencies, you will be well on your way to high performance.

Decentralize the Transformation

If you were to take a look at the transformation backlog for most agility champions, it would probably include one or more of the following:

- Charter a center of excellence, so that experts are easy to find.
- Design and deliver a standardized training curriculum, so that we have consistent messaging.
- Run several pilots, so that we focus on early wins.
- Go big, so that the transformation yields results faster.

These all make sense. And yet, strangely, the data tells us these conventional strategies are actually the least effective. According to the latest DevOps research, there are consistent patterns that differentiate the highest performing digital organizations from the lowest.[4]

Organic over Organized

The temptation for a well-managed organization is to conduct a well-managed and efficient transformation. After all, isn't good leadership about keeping the organization from suffering un-needed churn? But the data says something else. Specifically, higher performers were half as likely to go with a big-bang trans-formation with top-down direction. Moreover, they were less likely to form a transformation center to draft and roll out an official playbook.

High performers don't go for a well-organized rollout of new ways of working. Instead, small teams are authorized to pull whatever resources they need to improve their results. Then they let those results draw support for spreading new practices fur-ther across the organization, one step at a time.

The more you think about it, the more it makes sense. Consider that the old way of doing things is what got us into the kind of mess that merits transformation in the first place. A habit of running fast, efficient projects means we avoid the creative exploration we need for more innovation. A tradition of defining the new official universal process means we don't get that culture of highly engaged productivity.

To generate new levels of impact, we need to consider that the next level of answers will not come from us. It will come from them.

Communities over Centers

A key question around change is how to spread knowledge in a way that is both scalable and sustainable. It turns out those conventional approaches of classroom training programs and formal centers of excellence are more associated with the *lower* performers.

There are a few reasons for this. First, the center of excellence (COE) becomes a bottleneck for deploying needed expertise. You can add more people to the COE, but that doesn't scale nearly as fast as you need the transformation to happen. Second, it moves expertise away from doing work to merely advising work. The closer expertise is to work being done, the more likely staff are able to physically see what good looks like. Finally, a COE formalizes the divide between those who know and those who don't. This can create an unhealthy us-versus-them dynamic, undermining the culture aspect of a transformation.

Instead, high performers disseminate knowledge through informal communities of practice. These are meet-ups or chat rooms or webinars, where relevant examples, tips, and practices are swapped among the staff most motivated to spread them. These communities are authorized and supported by leadership, but the content, format, and audiences are wholly self-organized by staff on the ground. As a result, the change is magnetically attracted to those who are most motivated to adopt it.

Intentional over Incidental

It might be easy to misread these patterns as a directive for leaders to "get out of the way" and "let them fend for themselves." However, researchers make a very clear distinction: "Transformation is not a passive phenomenon. . . . High performers favor strategies that create community structures at both low and high levels of the organization."[5] This implies successful organic grassroots transformations are informed with a clear vision of what success looks like, rather than an ad hoc hope and a prayer.

For example, most organizations use pilot projects to generate momentum. However, a key difference is *how* the pilot projects are framed. Higher performers were much more likely to design their pilots either as a template for other teams to follow or as a breeding ground of new change leaders to deploy further into the organization. By contrast, lower performers were 156 percent more likely to see their pilot projects stall out and die, because they were merely tactical in nature.

That means pilots should be chartered to answer specific questions ("How do we, at this company, slice our project into smaller incremental deliveries?") and build new skills ("Let's learn ways to get our sponsors more actively engaged in these projects"), which can be leveraged further in the organization.

We still need to discover our new way of working. It's just that those answers should come from the cauldron of practice, proven on the ground, by passionate staff and leadership in our organization, rather than a playbook of techniques copied from some glossy textbooks. If our vision of agility is distorted and diluted in order to become more pervasive and impactful, that is worth it. Broad hybrid agility is better than beautiful siloed agility.

Here's the question. Is it about agile? Or is it about your agile? If you want a broader impact, you have to invite other people to the table, and when that happens, it will change the agile you have—which is the point. Is it about your agile, or is it about what the organization can do? Those are two different things.

Broad hybrid agility is better than beautiful siloed agility.

Give Away Your Position

Eventually, when we go about changing an organization, there will come a time when roles will need to change as well. Period. There's no avoiding it. Fundamentally, an organization is an amalgamation of people, all serving in different capacities.

Consider your current organization. It's perfectly optimized to deliver the results you're currently getting. To change those results, you have to change the organization, which means you have to change the role definitions of the people in the organization. Here are a few considerations.

Changes to the Project Manager Role

Without question, the most common conflict around role definitions in the agile conversation is around the role of the project manager. The traditional understanding of project manager is one who defines and follows heavyweight rigid processes, serves as the center of gravity for all project activity, and guides the execution of work according to a plan that is not permitted to change according to reality.

Around the turn of the century, the rising popularity of the Scrum framework introduced an innovative reconfiguration of the project manager into three distinct roles: a product owner who make business decisions, the project team that makes all the technical decisions, and the funny-named Scrum Master who uses various facilitation and collaboration techniques to help everyone be successful.

The intent was to (1) remove a singular decision maker as a bottleneck and (2) prevent the temptation that position invites for a directive and stifling style of leadership. However, as Scrum grew into the single most practiced agile framework,[6] the unexpected side effect was to disrupt the entire profession of project management. Today, leaders can hear experts declare offhandedly, "Agility requires using Scrum, which has no project manager, therefore project managers have no place in achieving agility." Although we can understand the human tendency to focus on superficial details like job titles, the result is the PM role evolved.

In 2015, the Project Management Institute introduced the talent triangle,[7] which placed a new expectation on project managers: not only are you expected to have knowledge and skill in work management processes, you are now also expected to bring a full tool kit of soft skills and a complete complement of business skills. Put simply, the role had expanded to incorporate those skills that Scrum has popularized. Project managers were now expected to fill a broader and more diversified definition. Rather than serving as process police, project managers were now asked to serve wherever they were needed.

But the changes have not stopped. At the time of this book's writing, I am also volunteering on the development team for the latest version of the ANSI standard for project management, the PMBOK® Guide—Seventh Edition. This latest edition will be based on new research into a further expansion of the role of project manager, as one that looks beyond the work at hand and considers the context of the work as well.

One thing is sure. Any roles your organization currently has around coordinating work are now under pressure. Achieving agility means being ready to redefine any of those roles.

Changes to the Line Manager Role

In his hilarious memoir *The Year Without Pants*,[8] Scott Berkun tells the story of becoming the first manager hired at Wordpress.com, the technology running the vast majority of blogs in the world. As you can imagine, this is a company that was built on innovation and resistant to any of the traps of conventional business as usual. So imagine when a career-long management author and speaker is invited to corral a group of globally distributed hotshot creatives and engineers. It's the perfect backdrop for a sitcom, but it's also a platform for deep learning. Some of the gems that I enjoyed in the book include:

- "For all my planning, scheming, and influencing as a team lead, sometimes talent, chaos, and chemistry are all you need for good work."
- "Organizations become bureaucratic as soon as people define their job around a specific rule, or feature, rather than a goal."
- "The same ego that drives grand leaders defeats them in the end because they can't accept the notion that someone will replace them."
- "The most dangerous tradition we hold about work is that it must be serious and meaningless."
- "While money provides status, status doesn't guarantee meaning."

Those insights are leading to an overarching trend in changes for the corporate manager. Google experimented with removing its managers, and when that turned into a galactic disaster, they brought them back and simply redefined the role.[9] Accenture and Deloitte have joined several companies in the trend to abolish annual performance appraisals.[10] Today's workplace is seeing an unprecedented degree of change in what it means to be a supervisor, a boss, or a manager of other people. Examples include:

- Your value is no longer in your expertise. You will be asked to manage people smarter than you.
- You are no longer the single point of contact for your team. You will be asked to encourage more direct staff collaboration across departments.
- You're no longer the only mentor available to your staff. Your advice will be augmented by various coaches from HR and other departments.

These are not absolutes, but they are very real trends. The specifics impacting your role will vary from one organization to another. The key point is to be willing to bend.

Changes to the Specialist Role

Years ago, a software engineer could get by with a very narrow specialty. "I am a Java developer," someone could say proudly, boldly, and knowing that would give them a strong career advantage. Today, many specialist roles have expanded into multiskilled disciplines:

- **Software engineers.** With the advent of Web 2.0 and subsequently the DevOps movement, more and more organizations are looking for the "full stack developer." In the past, a software engineer could specialize in database technologies versus user interface technologies versus integration technologies. In today's world, much of the mechanics that we are used to doing by hand are being automated. They create both the opportunity and the expectation for a technologist to diversify beyond a single specialty.

- **Social media staffers.** When we started posting our ideas online, the only thing you needed to know was how to use a web browser. Today, content creators are expected to have the visual creativity of a photographer, the text scrolling and skimming abilities of a researcher, the performance energy of an actor, and the conversion rates of a salesperson. Today's social media professional does much more than just type and send.

The bottom line is this: Those who work in the digital space are expected to be more versatile than ever before. Gone are the days when you could say, "That's not my job." In today's fast-paced world, the expectation is that professionals can innovate their skill set just as much as they can innovate the product they're working on.

Case Study: Reimagining the CEO Seat

The Scrum Alliance is the largest trade association in the world dedicated to organizational agility. In 2017, they were going through a leadership crisis. Board member Lisa Hershman was serving as interim CEO while an executive search committee was looking for her long-term replacement. After looking at several candidates, the conversation turned inward, and the board began asking some deeper questions. According to chairman Eric Engelmann, they started asking, "What if there was another way to think about this position? What if the job actually required more than one person? And what if that structure could look more like the [distributed leadership model in the] Scrum teams we're helping so many other companies and organizations build?"[11]

In September 2018, Howard Sublett was announced as the Chief Product Owner, focusing externally on the strategic vision for the organization. A few months later, Melissa Boggs was introduced as Chief Scrum Master, who serves internally on organizational growth and culture and fosters their ongoing transformation. Engelmann explains the theory, saying, "Together they fulfill the primary executive role in the organization. This approach was intended to help Scrum Alliance live the Scrum values deeply, even through our organizational design."

But that was just a beginning. Together Sublett and Boggs have been publicly sharing their challenges, insights, and experiments on a dedicated blog.[12] Recent milestones include:

- Team Swarm Days, in which teams spend an entire day collaborating on the same goal until it is complete
- Seeking and hiring culture: add talent in one day through an all-day series of designated activities called "Agile Hiring Events"
- Reorganizing into community-centric interdisciplinary teams, each a composite of competencies in IT, Marketing, Education, Support, and Community

By reimagining the senior executive position, the organization's transformation has hit a new inflection point.

If transformation means the most important role in an organization needs to be reexamined, that means any role might need to change in order to achieve agility. Granted, your mileage will vary. But the truth is pervasive: your role is constraining agility, whether it's the constraints of the silo you lead or the constraints of your job description.

Summary

In this chapter, we've explored the problem of impact. By being the first in the organization to launch forward into agility:

- **Understand expectations versus reality.** The changes you've made may have improved your department's professional excellence and discipline, but your localized improvements may not be having any impact on the bottom line yet.
- **Give away your agility**, so it can grow beyond your own physical limitations.
- **Give away your position**, so you can have more influence than ever before.

Is it about agility, or is it about *your* agility? Wrestling through that tension will allow you to find the untapped agility lying dormant in your organization.

CHAPTER 4

Throw the Textbook Away

*In theory there is no difference between theory and
practice, while in practice there is.*
—*Benjamin Brewster, 1882*

M ike knew a big move was needed.

The transformation at a century-old publishing company was stuck. Mike Anderson was asked to take it over and evolve it to the next phase. When he joined the firm, he started his discovery with several conversations, meetings, and reviews. He noticed some very helpful things had already been done. The technology group had reorganized into small multiskilled teams. They had aligned to an organizational cadence of working in consistent two-week cycles. They had even flattened the organization over several years, removing several layers of bureaucracy. But one problem was popping up over and over: The agile job titles got in the way.

Over the last twenty years, the strangely titled Scrum Master role has emerged as an established position in organizations wanting to accelerate team delivery and improvement.[1] It was envisioned as a facilitative master of ceremonies for a given work team, encouraging collaboration and focus. The official definition says,

> The Scrum Master is a servant-leader for the Scrum Team. . . . The Scrum Master helps everyone change [their] interactions to maximize the value created by the Scrum Team.

It could be described as an empowerment and improvement specialist embedded on the product team itself. The good news is that the industry has seen enough value in the role to where there are thousands of "Scrum Master" job postings the world over.

Yet, ironically, many in the industry misunderstand the role to be the process policeman for an organization. Many of these facilitators would judge their value on the degree of textbook perfection with which the team performs the Scrum framework. They would focus their energies on the process checklist (fifteen-minute stand-up, lessons-learned meetings, well-formatted backlogs), rather than how well they were thriving or evolving.

This was Mike's problem. He saw a lot of process policemen at his office, where dogma prevented experimentation and improvement. In his role as the transformation lead, he would intervene with some powerful questions: "After the process audit, what do you do next? You're holding these stand-up and retrospective meetings, but you're never teaching people why we actually hold them. How are you really improving these teams?"

His tough-love challenges would inspire some initial agreement from them and a commitment to change. But very quickly those empowerment specialists went back to old enforcement habits. It was time to shift perspectives by eliminating the distraction. No more Scrum Masters. Mike decided to keep the people and eliminate the old titles. Keep the team-level change agents but radically deviate their role from the established definition.

It worked. A few months after removing the job title associated with fostering collaboration, he was seeing *more* collaboration on the ground.

The Problem with Practices

In this chapter, we will explore a recurring pattern leaders experience on their path to agility. We will learn that much of what you've been told is hype. We will systematically deconstruct and debunk the most conventional advice about building high-performing, innovative, collaborative organizations. Specifically, the pattern goes like this:

- **The Boost.** Yes, it was good to install best practices.
- **The Barrier.** And yet, they're doing it wrong.
- **The Rebound.** So throw the textbook away.

The Pattern of Untapped Practices

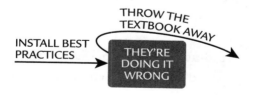

The Boost: Yes, It Was Good to Install Best Practices

Good decision—let's use some practices that are out there in the industry. They've been proven by thousands of organizations and come with a corpus of literature and tools to support their use.

Leaders Install Best Practices

Ted Team Lead	Maria Manager	Emmit Executive
"I'd like us to start formatting our specifications in the Given-When-Then template because it really helped at my last job."	"I'd like us to display our work on a public task board because a conference talk showed it can improve teamwork."	"I'd like us to charter funding review boards because our strategy consultant says it will help to kill bad projects."

Moreover, we gain credibility by using a modern management approach that didn't involve reinventing the wheel. Put simply, best practices are a good idea.

The Barrier: And Yet, They're Doing It Wrong

We get frustrated because our teams are not rising to the challenge. The process or framework should be yielding more benefit, but our staff are either struggling with them, resisting proper execution, or just plain confused. It's not sticking. Why is this so hard for them?

If you've tried these modern practices, then maybe you've run into one of these examples of poor agility:

- The daily stand-up takes forever, disrupting productivity.
- That "empowered" team still defers to their manager, who serves as a bottleneck.
- The work items are too big and keep slipping to the next deadline.
- Teams are interrupted with work that sneaks in through back channels.

Leaders Struggle with Poor Practices

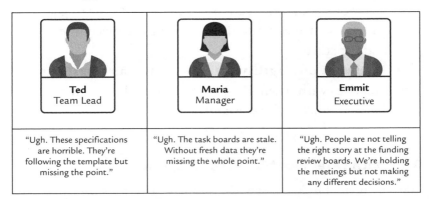

Ted Team Lead	Maria Manager	Emmit Executive
"Ugh. These specifications are horrible. They're following the template but missing the point."	"Ugh. The task boards are stale. Without fresh data they're missing the whole point."	"Ugh. People are not telling the right story at the funding review boards. We're holding the meetings but not making any different decisions."

- People incur double overhead by practicing new methods on top of the legacy practices already in place.
- Lessons-learned meetings repeat the same problems each month, with no meaningful change.
- The teams don't understand how to format their backlog or documentation, so you do it for them.

This happens because you have what I call "right team, wrong agile." Just because it worked in your last environment doesn't mean your current environment is similar enough for it to work this time. Just because that case study highlighted a fancy technique for your sector doesn't mean your team is ready to try it.

The Rebound: So Throw the Textbook Away

So what do you do? You explore how to modify those sacrosanct systems to address the reality on the ground.

- **The data does not match the dogma**. A little digging reveals startling secrets that debunk some common convictions about agile practices.

- **Find your legs.** We will introduce a set of simple questions your team can use to figure out how to get past the confusion and difficulty of agile mechanics and get started.
- **Find your own agility.** It turns out we can adjust our practices with intent. Doing so avoids diluting their value and better fits the context.

The Data Does Not Match the Dogma

Earlier in the book, we saw that agility generates improvement more often than not. So the next question would naturally be "What did you do to achieve those results?"

The experts, champions, authors, and consultants would all say those successes are wholly contingent on the proper implementation of best practices, proven frameworks, and robust technologies. However, the latest survey from practitioners across the world says something different.[2]

- **Unconventional speed.** While 63 percent report better speed of delivery, barely half of the same group are doing so with frequent releases. A meaningful number of organizations are somehow delivering faster *without* delivering frequently.
- **Meetings are not enough.** More than 80 percent practice a full suite of formal collaboration meetings, from daily stand-ups to short-term planning, to public reviews and retrospectives. But only 69 percent are experiencing *any* organizational benefits at all. For many people following the most common practices, something else is missing.
- **Customers not required.** The standard advice for improving customer satisfaction is to embed a dedi-

cated customer, sponsor, or product owner into a delivery team. Yet somehow nearly 64 percent of teams experience improved alignment between sponsors and teams, when only 57 percent of them have that required role in place. Apparently, when it comes to making customers happy, their involvement is helpful but not mandatory.

- **Poker isn't the point.** Among the most hotly debated practices is that of team-based estimation of work assignments. Referred to as "planning poker," it may take more time, but asking the whole team to assess their workload will be more accurate compared to the sole expert judgment of a senior team member. And yet, while nearly two-thirds practice the technique, only 52 percent experienced the increased predictability it was supposed to yield.

We see there are both hits and misses that happen, despite the use or non-use of the very agile methods we advocate for. How is this possible?

Find Your Legs

The seduction of best practices comes from the very real fact that they've worked so well for so many people. There is value and substance to them. However, my reality often doesn't cooperate with your history.

Let's say you do believe in the power of more collaboration, more creativity, more engagement, more flexibility. Let's say your boss approves of you inserting Scrum, Kanban, or DevOps to achieve that vision, but he wants a roadmap for what this initiative will look like. So you do some research and come up with a plan that shows concrete milestones. It even comes complete with a hockey stick chart that shows performance moving up and to the right.

It turns out the path to excellence is a bit bumpier than that. In fact, most change journeys follow a reliable pattern of pain before we get to the promise of a better tomorrow. The truth often looks less like a hockey stick and more like what scientists call the J-curve. It describes a phenomenon we all know simply as this: it gets worse before it gets better.

It gets worse before it gets better.

The J Curve of Change

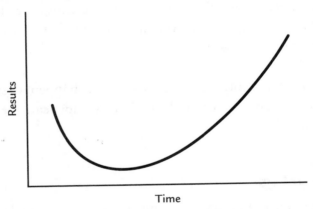

Here are some fields where the pattern has been identified:

- In economics, the curve plots financial returns over time. Whether it's the profitability of a product or the capital gains of an index fund, the short-term costs run pull the curve down. It's only over time that gains are recognized.
- In geopolitics, author Ian Bremmer discovered the pattern describes the fluctuation of nation-state stability

(Y-axis) over a progressively increasing degree of openness (X-axis).[3] When relatively stable totalitarian regimes explore certain human virtues like democracy, freedom of the press, and civil rights, things initially get worse (e.g., the Arab Spring). It's only when those societies move further into those virtues that hope begins to emerge.

- In family therapy, author Virginia Satir used this to illustrate how change impacts personal fulfillment over time. She follows the "change curve" through four sequential stages, from status quo to resistance to chaos to integration.[4]

If this pattern has economic, social, and emotional elements, then it's no surprise that we see it appear in organizational transformation as well. As we venture into our transformation, things get awkward, different, frustrating, even painful. Only over time do the changes settle into a new stability. When it comes to injecting positive change into the status quo, be prepared for the roller coaster.

It's Easy to Blame the ScrumButs

Let's go back to that Scrum framework. It is easily one of the most popular frameworks in the innovation, DevOps, and agile movements.[5] Unfortunately, beginners tend to make mistakes. Lots of them. Either they don't fully understand the method or they flex some of the guidelines intended to be very fixed. Instead of just letting beginners go through their growing pains, some thought leaders have succumbed to their frustration, and refer to these beginners by a handy epithet, the ScrumBut:

[Scrum] is designed to provide the desired benefits and address predictable recurring problems. A ScrumBut retains the problem while modifying Scrum to make it invisible so that the dysfunction is no longer a thorn in the side of the team.

A ScrumBut has a particular syntax: (ScrumBut) (Reason)(Workaround)

ScrumBut Examples:

"(We use Scrum, but) (having a Daily [stand-up meeting] every day is too much overhead), (so we only have one per week)."

"(We use Scrum, but) (sometimes our managers give us special tasks), (so we don't always have time to meet our definition of done)."[6]

The implication is that those who modify the framework reveal less of a genuine wrestling with a different way of working and more of a flaw of personal character.

But what if we begin daily stand-ups the only way we know how? With formal agendas, too many participants, and a cumbersome teleconference system? Are we weak in the knees or just getting started?

But what if we haven't figured out the bottlenecks in our delivery process? Does extending the maximum one-month work cycles into two-month cycles reflect a commitment to the past or just a symptom of problems we're figuring out?

But what if it takes me more than a year to unlearn twenty years of habitually interrupting my staff? Am I an evil supervisor or merely beginning my journey of self-awareness?

A Google search for "ScrumBut" yields well over 100,000 results for such a funny word. Apparently, it's quite common to get frustrated with imperfection. The problem is that frustration can turn into judgment. By using a humorous label to highlight noncompliance, we may actually be discouraging people who need help, not criticism.

But Isn't Growth the Whole Point?

If you feel, like me, that this is a bit judgmental, the good news is we are not alone. Blogger Cliff "The Clever PM" Gilley makes the point that the concept of growing *into* high performance means not starting *at* high performance:

> "ScrumBut" implies perfection at the start. . . . If the direction that these people are getting is that Scrum is an all-or-nothing proposition (which is precisely what "ScrumBut" does), then the change agents who are trying to make incremental changes have yet another hurdle to overcome, one tossed into the fray by the very people whom we want to provide support to our efforts.[7]

He makes the fairly obvious point that, in order to something well, we must first do it poorly. Not merely doing the practices themselves poorly but also doing the learning, the evolution, the incremental improvement poorly.

Moreover, the end state of high performance often ends up looking quite different from the textbook set of practices we've all come to admire. This is the additional point made by Jurgen Appelo, TEDx speaker and author of the breakthrough book *Management 3.0*:

> A process or method is a description of behavior. Scrum describes how a development team *might* be able to successfully deliver software to its environment. But because *optimal* behavior is a function of internal structure and external environment, the real optimal method always depends on the team's structure and environment.
>
> In short: the optimal method will always be an adaptation. . . .

It's OK to say, "We do Scrum, but we don't do stand-ups because there are only two of us, and we already communicate all day."[8]

Given that most professionals will already have exposure to so many established techniques, a strong case can be made to just use them. In fact, several of your team members will already have deep experience using some or all of the techniques out there. Meanwhile, with so much literature already available, doing anything else might inspire blowback from your teams:

"Why is there no automation in this department?"
"Why are these requirements not written in the user story format?"
"Why do we not have a Scrum Master running this meeting?"

So how can we take advantage of those tacit assets without the inevitable judgment, frustration, and pain of some people and some teams just starting out?

Crawl, Walk, Run

We've already discussed the dynamics of growth on a personal level and a team level. There is a rich body of research on adult development and team maturity, but it's not necessary to read it to understand this commonsense principle: you can't be perfect the first day you do something.

- **Crawl.** Initially, we try a technique as best we can. We will violate several recommended guidelines and get only marginal benefit from the technique. It feels awkward but doable.
- **Walk.** Gradually, we get better. We remove the barriers, the overhead, the confusion that held us back in the

beginning. As we get better, we get more benefit.
It looks and feels good, but we know it's not ideal yet.
• **Run.** Eventually, we get pretty good. We meet or exceed
the recommended guidelines and thrive together.

Crawl Walk Run

That's it. We give ourselves permission to start with what we can
and make a commitment to grow into it. Here are two examples
from real teams in the real world of how violating best practices
can actually represent growth.

Example: Ted Figures Out the Daily Stand-Up

• **Crawl.** Initially, I called our fifteen-person team together for daily stand-ups. The manager supported the move but annoyingly wanted a formal agenda, just like any other meeting. It's a grueling forty minutes, but we all feel more confident sharing today what we previously had to wait to share at the weekly status meeting.
• **Walk.** Gradually, we learned how to be more informal and more focused on raising issues and deferring solutions to follow-up conversations. Once in a while we get stuck in a rabbit hole, but overall it feels much smoother at a more reliable twenty minutes.

- **Run.** Eventually, the group decided there was just too much going on for one team. We broke into two smaller teams, and now it feels much more focused. It's taken us several months, but we've learned enough about working together that we can check in for five minutes and get right to work.

Example: Maria Figures Out the Public Task Board

Maria
Manager

- **Crawl.** Initially, leadership asked us to track project deliverables on a public task board, something he calls a Kanban, a technique from Lean Manufacturing. These are the most strategic things sponsors are asking for and the reason we're getting yelled at. Meanwhile, we're pretty good at closing ad hoc support tickets quickly, so we leave them off the board to keep it clean and uncluttered. We do feel micromanaged by this tool, but our executive is demanding that something changes.
- **Walk.** Gradually, we realized those invisible support tickets take up most of our time, so we added them on the board too. Meanwhile, the project deliverables are blocked by external dependencies, so we added a stage called "dead in the water." It looks messier, but at least we are finally starting to see why things are taking so long.
- **Run.** Eventually, the board became too cluttered, so one team member tried color-coding items on the board. It was a breakthrough. We can see there was just too much going on. It's taken us several months, but the visibility has helped us fix bottlenecks and build trust with management.

Find Your Own Agility

We've been told that if you want to create empowerment and engagement on your teams, you follow a specific proven set of steps:

1. Form a team.
2. Tell them they are empowered.
3. Watch the magic happen.

Empowered self-organizing work teams are the center of most agile methods. If you want high performance, you ask your people what *they* think we should do to help them get better.

But one submarine commander did something completely different. He didn't ask staff. He asked the middle managers instead.

In his book *Turn the Ship Around!* former U.S. Navy captain L. David Marquet shares an inspiring case study.[9] He walks us through his messy journey of transforming the worst submarine in the navy into the best in the navy.

So how did he do it? He had to find *his* agility, a collaborative operative system specific to his boat. So he asked all his noncommissioned officers (NCOs, whom he calls middle managers) what control meant to them. They said it was about paid time off (PTO). Apparently, at the time there were four layers of PTO approvals. If anyone wanted to take a day off, and the team lead approved it, that wasn't enough. It had to go to the junior officer, then the executive officer, and then the captain himself.

But if the original team lead's decisions were supported by the officers, then he could now control who was going to backfill, who was the backup, who was going to cross-train the backfill and the backup. The authority to do one thing sparked the freedom and creativity to do several other things. Rather than just follow the literature, Marquet found their keystone, their linchpin, *their* agility.

Agility Requires Tailoring Practices

Much has been written in the project and product worlds about "tailoring" processes and practices, based on the work being done. Let's pause for a moment to take a look at some key points. The 2017 ANSI standard for project management defines it officially as follows:[10]

> Determining the appropriate combination of processes, inputs, tools, techniques, outputs, and the life cycle phases to manage a project is referred to as "tailoring" the application of the knowledge [of project management].

That's a fancy way of saying that each organization should customize its approach to delivering work based on the specific dynamics and demands of the environment. Moreover, these adjustments are not optional. The guide goes on to say:

> Tailoring is necessary because each project is unique; not every process, tool, input, or output identified in [this standard] is necessary.

Now if you think that point is only for traditional project management and has nothing to do with Agility, then you would be mistaken.

The original Agile Manifesto closes out its declaration of values and principles with this very topic:

> At regular intervals, the team reflects on how to become more effective, then tunes and adjusts its behavior accordingly.

That's the conclusion, the climax, the final word. Kind of important.

So whether you come from a formal standards perspective (project management) or a more informal values-based perspective (Agile Manifesto), the expectation is the same: modify how you do your work, based on the situation at hand.

Put another way, if you believe in continuous improvement, then by definition whatever practices you are using are not optimal. If you are still using that fancy new management method strictly out of the box, then you are simultaneously neither compliant with international standards nor consistent with the spirit of agility. Not adjusting your practices is a double-fail.

The Three Ps: Pain, Purpose, Pivot

Unfortunately, there is almost zero guidance on how to go about tailoring effectively. Much of the literature in place today strongly advises that you do it but offers no filters, guardrails, or tips for doing so. That's a problem, because if we don't make the right adjustments we can get some very unwelcome side effects.

- We don't change it enough and still struggle unnecessarily.
- We change it too much and lose all the benefit we're trying to get.

How do we customize our practices without diluting their potency or even making things worse? We need to offer people a viable alternative beyond all-or-nothing. To do that, we can walk through a simple set of questions to figure out some degree of doing things better:

1. **Listen to their pain.** Ask the team *what* is the specific frustration, difficulty, challenge they would face if we were to use a given technique.

2. **Explain the purpose.** Share the underlying principle of *why* we recommend that technique. What is the intended benefit?

3. **Solicit a pivot.** Ask the team *how* might we adjust the technique so that we could get at least some of that benefit.

Here is how the process works in real life.

Example: Ted Wrestles with Global Teams

Ted
Team Lead

- **Ted's Pain.** "Our coach says face-to-face conversation is best, but our team is spread across four cities, a total of twelve hours apart. We're okay with staying up late for a team meeting once a week. But doing that every day is unreasonable, let alone multiple times a day for so-called 'collaboration' time. In fact, a couple of us barely speak English."

Three Steps for Tailoring Practice

1. Pain

Name the frustration, difficulty, challenge posed by a given technique.

⬇

2. Purpose

Share the underlying principle of that technique.

⬇

3. Pivot

Adjust the technique to get some of that benefit.

- **A colleague explains the Purpose.** "Remember, the purpose of face time is to improve communication and team building."
- **Ted's Pivot.** "Well, in that case, at least the team building part seems easy. We love our team chat tool; it gets a lot of activity. Maybe we could create a 'personal' thread where we can post fun things to get to know each other better. Then we can limit our video chats to some reasonable timeslots, without losing the personal connection we would get through more face time."

Example: Maria Wrestles with Regulated, Life-Critical Environments

Maria
Manager

- **Maria's Pain.** "Experts say documents are wasteful. But we build medical devices. Those documents are how we pass compliance audits."
- **A colleague explains the Purpose.** "Remember, the emphasis of 'working product' over 'comprehensive documentation' is to avoid distractions that waste time. I'm sure you can think of how to adjust your documentation practices to save time, without compromising the safety of the work you do."
- **Maria's Pivot.** "Well, much of our time is spent using our specifications to convey designs to the builders. But talking is faster than typing. We could accelerate knowledge sharing by including the designers and auditors in our meetings more frequently. Then writing the compliance documents will be more focused on meeting regulations, rather than directing the actual work. That might improve quality and speed, without

losing any of the documentation the government requires. Let's try this as an experiment for one subset of the overall product."

Example: Emmit Wrestles with Organizational Silos

Emmit
Executive

- **Emmit's Pain.** "DevOps says we form multiskilled, full-life-cycle teams. But our company has a very strict hierarchy. Any teams we form will be within departmental skill sets and follow the chain of command for any decisions."

- **A colleague explains the Purpose.** "Remember, the purpose of teams is to bring all the needed perspectives closer together to accelerate decisions and knowledge. You do *not* need a reorg to start your journey. You can keep the existing org structures, and add a few adjustments to bring more alignment more quickly."

- **Emmit's Pivot.** "We've had success in the past with 'tiger teams' staffed with representatives from impacted departments. We could also have them meet weekly around the program dashboard. We'll be careful to strike the right balance of visualizing progress, without exposing any embarrassing information on the board. That's not consistent with what our DevOps trainer said, but it might get us started."

These are just a few examples—your mileage will vary. The point is a little agility is better than none. Regardless of where you work, there is already plenty of improvement lying dormant in your project. Take these simple steps, host a collaborative conversation, and warp those best practices to achieve a little more untapped agility.

Mike's Success Story

Recall Mike, our transformation leader at the publishing company we learned about in the beginning of this chapter. He was frustrated by his collaboration facilitators, Scrum Masters, viewing their role as process police. His move was to keep the same Scrum framework in place but remove the formal master-of-ceremonies role that was causing so much drama. In my follow-up conversations with Mike, I asked him how his experiment was going.

Have there been any consequences of removing the established practice of a formal Scrum Master role?
One of the new frustrations I'm hearing is that the change put into limbo those who were holding the title. Despite our detailed transition plan and communication efforts, they didn't understand the alternative roles we offered them. We said, "You have to flip into another role: project manager, product owner, technical leader, etc. You tell me what you want to do and where you think you would fit the best on your team or in the organization. You pick your destiny, and we will be here to support you, since we're making this change." Yet, despite our efforts to make the transition seamless, it has still been difficult. It's because we removed what they knew. The industry says to use this method, it *must* be done this way, and we've violated that prescription.

Fair enough, but what has the change allowed you to achieve as an organization?
Firstly, we removed the false conflict with those holding "project manager" titles. A lot of the Scrum Masters do

have project management backgrounds. And yet it was always Scrum Masters against project managers, bickering over where lines were drawn. But they all do the same thing: help projects be more successful. Now we don't fight over that anymore, because the artificial distinction is gone, and surprise, surprise, the teams are still working autonomously.

Second, the business sponsors are working a lot more fluently with technology teams now. Before, teams were discouraged from interacting directly with business sponsors. Sponsors would make decisions and drive them down to the product owner, who then transmitted that information to the teams. That product owner role became a wall we didn't even notice. The teams only ever heard a watered-down version of what their business counterparts were dealing with. So by ditching the conventional Scrum roles as they're traditionally understood, the hope is to create more alignment. After the changes we made, it was more acceptable and encouraged for business and execution teams to interact directly.

Bottom line, it wasn't pretty, but it removed our biggest barrier to getting to the next level of high-performance collaboration.

Summary

In this chapter, we've challenged the conventional understanding of modern practices like Scrum, Lean Startup, Kanban, DevOps, and so forth. In the pursuit of textbook perfection, we've learned:

- **The data does not match the dogma.** The latest research reveals that much of what experts demand as mandatory actually isn't.

- **Find your legs.** Growth requires doing those practices poorly before we do them well.
- **Find your own agility.** Context requires tailoring and adjusting. Use the three Ps (Pain, Purpose, Pivot) to experiment with intentional modifications of established practices.

The path to higher performance often does start with proven frameworks, established techniques, and known methods. But eventually you will have to break them in order to find your untapped agility.

CHAPTER 5

Master "No"

> People think focus means saying yes to the thing you've got
> to focus on. But that's not what it means at all. It means
> saying no to the hundred other good ideas that there are.
> —*Steve Jobs*

Luis was knee-deep in a transformation, and his patience was being tested.

The scene was Lonely Planet. For decades, the company has been one of the most celebrated brands in the travel business. Yet, in mid-2018, they were struggling internally.

For the previous few years, their very creative-minded CEO had run amuck, percolating new product ideas every week. Projects were not making any progress, because newer, cooler ideas would get more traction. Staff were exhausted from being pulled around in so many directions, and the bottom line was not looking good.

Eventually, the firm's billionaire owner had had enough. He removed the CEO and asked digital strategy consultant Luis Cabrera to assess the situation and introduce some stability.

As Luis started his discovery, the issues started piling on: managers complained they were paid less than their staff; the org chart had enough layers to rival large bureaucracies; leaders were jockeying for the empty slot at the top; the technologies in place limited innovation; the team practices were inconsistent and unstructured. The sheer volume was daunting. Jobs were at stake. And you have a billionaire watching your next move. The pressure was on. What do you do?

One thing was clear: he could not repeat the same fragmented, frantic approach of the previous leadership. He would *not* do everything at once. For many of the fixes that were needed, he would have to offer a short-term "No, not now."

Paradoxically, to get everything done, he would have to resist the pressure to do everything. And it worked. Here's why.

The Problem with Progress

In this chapter, we look at another reason why your transformation is stuck: the overcommitted workload. Here's how it happens:

- **The Boost.** Yes, you seized all the right opportunities.
- **The Barrier.** And yet, you're always behind on deadlines and expectations.
- **The Rebound.** So now, master how to say no.

The Pattern of Untapped Progress

The Boost: Yes, You Seized All the Right Opportunities

Success comes from bold moves. It's good practice. Whether it's internal influence, more features, or more products, nobody gets ahead by resting on their butts. You're either moving or not moving.

Leaders Seize Opportunities

The Barrier: And Yet, You're Always Behind on Deadlines and Expectations

Oddly, the more aggressive we are, the more dates we slip, the more our sponsors complain, the more work we have to do. The more we do, the more we're behind.

Leaders Struggle with Limited Progress

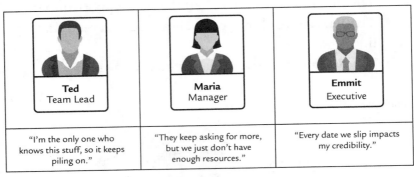

The Rebound: So Now, Master How to Say No

The problem is you're overcommitted. Period. The solution is focus. To get to the destination sooner, start saying no to all those detours and distractions.

We need to build everything on the radar, faster than reasonable. To do that, we need to be completely digital, lean, and agile. By yesterday. For that to happen, we need everyone to rise to the challenge.

To solve this dynamic, we need to move forward at the pace that matches who we are as an organization. That requires we learn how to say no to the three great sources of overcommitment:

- **Say no to delivering everything.** There is never a shortage of work to do. But the more work we do at once, the less capacity we have to transform the work itself. Reducing the daily load allows for more improvement.
- **Say no to transforming everything.** Some parts of the business need to be transformed first, but other parts can wait until later. Hold off changing too much at once.
- **Say no to you in everything.** High achievers see more opportunities than most and feel compelled to go after them. Knowing your tendencies and habits better can help in managing the personal backlog.

Master How to Say "No"

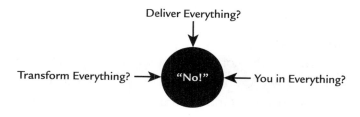

Say No to Delivering Everything

Executives are held to more performance goals each year. Sponsors are funding more projects. Competitors are disrupting our offerings. There's a ton of work to do and never enough money, people, or time to do it.

Then isn't it great we have agility? We live in the most innovative age of mankind. Shouldn't we be able to "do more with less"?

Well, that certainly fits the narrative. The State of Agile Report says practitioners are more likely than not to increase productivity (61 percent) and increase speed (63 percent).[1] Indeed, the most recent State of DevOps Report[2] says that, relative to the lowest performing digital organizations, the highest performing organizations deploy completed work to operations 106 times faster and recover from mistakes 2,604 times faster. The best-selling book on the Scrum framework explains how to get "twice the work in half the time."[3]

The expectation is this: agility means get more done faster.

Meanwhile, everyone's already busy. How do we build the airplane as we fly it? It turns into a crazy cycle where we eventually throw up our hands in despair and shout, "We are too busy doing work to get better at the work we do!" So the answer is to move in the opposite direction.

We are too busy doing work to get better at the work we do!

Kill More Projects

Of all the role model companies we look up to, Google sits on the throne of the digital kingdom. From YouTube to Gmail to Chrome to Android to Google Maps to Google Drive, they have number-one market share in half a dozen Internet products. Oh, yeah, and then there's that search thing too.

And yet, Google is also a graveyard of dead products. There were some that were around for years, such as Google Glass, Hangouts, and the Google Search Appliance. But for each of those almost-wins, there are several that did not last very long at all. KilledByGoogle.com is a fascinating website that lists products and services that are no longer offered or supported. The list includes such obscure gems as these:

- Dragonfly was going to fix search for Chinese censorship rules (lasted one year).
- Needlebase was a point-and-click Internet content organizer (lasted one year).
- NOOP was a programming language blending old world and new world computing (lasted three years).
- Buzz was a social media plug-in for Gmail (lasted two years).
- Writely was a web-based word processor (lasted one year).

The website goes on to detail almost 200 failed products. But how is that possible? How could a company be so successful when so many of their products fail? Because those products are killed before too much money is spent on them. They realize what techpreneur and creator of Innovation Games Luke Hohmann explains, "You don't have insufficient resources, you simply have an overabundance of good ideas."[4]

"You don't have insufficient resources, you simply have an overabundance of good ideas." — Luke Hohmann

---

First, we already have too much going at once. To trim the fat and get more efficient, we need to master artillery. In their book *Great by Choice*,[5] business authors Jim Collins and Morten T. Hansen explore how businesses succeeded during the Great Recession. One key technique: "Tracer bullets. Then cannonballs." Go small to find out where to go. Then go big to get there.

- **Stage 1 (Ideation).** In every organization, managers mobilize projects to achieve their annual goals. But what if we dispensed with those annual goals and instead considered all those projects merely potential ideas. What if we treated all ideas as initially equal in their unvalidated state, and allow them to compete for funding based solely on their merit. Let's say we collect 100 potential projects or products to invest in.
- **Stage 2 (Exploration).** For each idea, we invest a minimal amount of labor to seek data to confirm whether it has potential. Is there truly a need? Do we give it another round of funding? We use those first "tracer bullets" to see what lands where. Common sense tells us that of those 100 investments, maybe half will ever get around to running those tests.
- **Stage 3 (Validation).** With 50 sets of data, we can rack and stack which ones have promise. Then we can choose the top 25 candidates to see whether we can generate value at a larger scale. Can we have validate the business case? Is this the value we want, relative to our long-term vision? We narrow our aim and fire more targeted tracer bullets.
- **Stage 4 (Exploitation).** Eventually, we come to the survival of the top 2 or 5 or 10 fittest ideas. Now is when we switch from small bullet-sized experiments to firing the cannonball-sized investment.

Metered Funding Enables Lean Portfolios

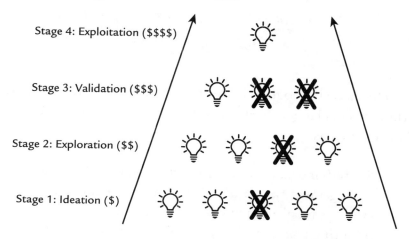

This same concept is formalized in the Lean Startup method as metered funding.[6] This is in contrast to the more common corporate tradition of entitlement funding. Traditionally, we fund every project and do them all at once. You get 5 million, you get 5 million, you get 5 million, and you get 5 million. All good? Call me back next year for your next round. Then we are shocked to discover that we need a lot of people to fire a cannonball, and we only have so many people. Moreover, all our best talent is needed on all those cannonballs.

Instead, we can use metered funding, which is doled out only to those projects that have proven their worth through several smaller experiments. All the other lower-value ideas, which would have normally been approved, are thrown by the wayside. This kind of organizational focus means more resources, more focus, more speed, more performance, more, more, more . . . all by doing fewer projects at once. You run this process continuously throughout the year, rather than a rigid annual cycle.

Hohmann offers another insight into high-performing organizations: "You can measure the maturity of your portfolio management by your project kill rate."

> *"You can measure the maturity of your portfolio management by your project kill rate."* — Luke Hohmann

This is how Google achieves its organizational focus.[7] With the focus in play, it can run all kinds of transformational experiments, such as:

- Simplifying a quarterly 41-point employee performance management system down to a leaner 5-point system every six months, saving tons of overhead.
- Adopting a provocative "pay unfairly" compensation model that retains their highest performers.
- Installing employee amenities that keep them happy and focused, ranging from onsite bike repairs to mobile haircuts to Take Your Parents to Work Day.

Consider that if Google staff were still supporting those 200 dead projects, they would be running so ragged they wouldn't be able to adopt or enjoy the transformations that make Google such a competitive place to work.

Kill more projects. Spend less money. You'll get things done faster, and you'll create room for teams for support the transformation you're striving for.

Say No to Transforming Everything

Transformation initiatives fail to achieve their goals for one of two reasons:

- **We didn't go far enough.** Our change needed to be safe and nonthreatening, so it was limited to pilots,

which yielded only short-term results. We addressed
that in chapter 3, "Give It Away."

- **We burned out.** Our change needed to be fast and
all-encompassing, so it was expanded prematurely to
cover everything, which caused confusion, frustration,
and cancellation. This is what we want to talk about
here.

Organizational change is hard. Too much of it at once merely
makes it harder. Here's how to limit the change.

Ration Your Ambition

Here's one I hear often. A leader catches the transformation
fever and declares, "By the end of the year, we are going to be
100 percent digital, 100 percent agile, 100 percent lean. Every
project, every department, every service." It's bold. Ambitious.
Future-oriented.

And it's a bad idea.

In 2012, Bansi Nagji and Geoff Tuff introduced the innovation ambition model, which differentiates three distinct regions:
core, adjacent, and transformational.

- **Core.** You have your core business. You're optimizing
existing offerings for existing consumers. This is where
you know what you know, you know how to win, and
you know where to play.
- **Adjacent.** Meanwhile, there are a handful of true
innovations, which add incremental products
and offerings to adjacent customers. These carry a
few more assumptions and are a little bit more
ambitious.
- **Transformational.** Then there's further out from your
core, where you kind of don't know how to win and you

don't know where to play. It's a new place, it's a different thing. And that's where your approach should be a lot more agile.

That's right, ladies and gentlemen; agility is not for everything. In fact, Nagji and Tuff's research found higher-performing companies (as measured by stock price) carried a recurring pattern: the portfolio should be 70 percent on your core products and your core business, 20 percent on adjacent, and 10 percent on transformation. The further out you are into crazy land, with new ventures and new spaces, the more innovative you need to be, the more risk you have financially. Conversely, the more stable and reliable your products, the less effective those innovation methods are.

Put another way, if only three out of ten products or programs are using Scrum/DevOps/Kanban methods, then you're following research-based innovation guidelines. Only 30 percent of your portfolio needs transformation.

Only 30 percent of your portfolio needs transformation.

Then I get the transformation purists rebutting: "Um, just because the outer regions incur more uncertainty doesn't mean the Core is off the hook! They also need a more digital, collaborative, adaptive way of working, even if just to consume new innovations." Fair enough. I will concede that general business agility is a new competitive necessity. But that does not mean the same full-scale transformation is worth the cost in every part of an organization. Context matters. Which leads us to a difficult question: When is agility worth it and when is it inappropriate? And how do we decide?

Agility Requires Investment

If you want the quick answer, here it is: Use agile/digital/innovation methods only when it's worth the investment. Agility is not for free. If you want to play, you have to pay the admission fee. Here's what that looks like:

- **Collaboration.** The Scaled Agile Framework is the most popular textbook model for organizational agility.[8] It's fundamentally designed to focus dozens or hundreds of employees around medium-term goals. To achieve that focus, the framework prescribes a ten-week cycle that consists of several collaboration events, ranging from fifteen-minute daily stand-ups all the way up to a two-day all-hands workshop. When you add it up, individual contributors spend a recommended average of 15 percent of their time in formally scheduled meetings.[9] That makes sense for large interrelated efforts that require continuous communication. But working on more smaller independent initiatives may not need that much.
- **Rework.** Building prototypes for customer feedback creates a stronger product with more alignment to market needs. It also invites adjustments and additions to the workload. That rework is a necessary part of the exploration of new customers and products, but it may not be needed for work that is already well known.
- **Allocation.** Most thought leaders recommend increasing productivity, quality, and morale by fully allocating each team member 100 percent to a single team working on a single stream of work. However, what is the likelihood that this month's highest priorities will 100 percent align to each and every staffer's skill

availability? Zero. That means every month there is at least some idle time. In theory, a little slack in workload for one or two people allows them to assist on other team activities, boosting teamwork and knowledge sharing. However, it may be hard to justify that intermittent idle time for every skill set on every project everywhere in the company.

All that work and time represent investment. Should we be investing that much in our transformational initiatives? Yes! Otherwise, we incur risk that undermines the entire venture. On the other hand, is that investment worth applying to operational, everyday, run-of-the-mill, no-surprises work in the core region? I doubt it. Rather, it makes the most sense to focus your transformational energies on your transformational regions.

Don't Ask Whether Agility, Ask How Much

Now that we know to focus our transformational energies to only some of the organization, we can make progress on evolving just those programs and products.

But isn't that inconsistent and confusing? How can we simultaneously have agility here, but not there? What kind of organization do we design to support multiple operating systems?

The Either-Or Approach

In recent years, the innovation-ambition matrix has been further elaborated by Gartner's bimodal framework for IT organizations.[10] It recommends the organization be governed by two exclusive management systems. Mode 1 is the marathon runner. It matches the core region in our innovation-ambition matrix, and optimizes management for areas that are more predictable and well understood. Mode 2 is the sprinter. It matches the adjacent and transformational regions. It's exploratory, experimenting to solve new problems and optimized for areas of uncertainty.

It's a logical construct, except it creates lots of problems. An article in *CIO* magazine highlights a few of them:[11]

- **The false free pass.** When leaders designate work streams as core/traditional/model, many interpret that as a waiver on having to do any improvement at all. Although collaborative team building, retrospectives, and strict priorities are associated with agility, those outcomes could have benefits everywhere.
- **Two options isn't enough.** Meanwhile, advocating a dual operating system directly implies a limit of two ways of working. Either all mode 1 projects are done exactly this way or all mode 2 projects are done exactly that way. This encourages a monolithic use of a given approach, without adjusting any elements to specific situations.
- **Mode 2, right now.** And if all our fast projects are to be run the same way, then it generates undue pressure to transform all those teams right away. Otherwise we can't support all the projects moving into that category.
- **Dependencies.** Meanwhile, a fast-slow division of the organization ignores the reality that many fast projects are dependent on slow projects, offering little guidance on how to reconcile that tension.
- **Team division.** Breaking up the organization into two modes creates an us-versus-them culture. The slow teams are envious of the cool stuff the others get to do, and the fast teams look down on the others for doing things the old way.

And so on, and so on. The either-or mindset is a recipe for headaches. Fortunately, there's another way.

The Hybrid Approach

Change is rarely instantaneous. It is more than just before and after. It evolves over time. For every person who quit smoking cold-turkey, there are plenty of others who have to cut down a little at a time. For every person who learns to ride a bicycle in a single lesson, there are those who wobble forward—walking, then peddling, then walking again before ultimately settling into a groove.

When scaling change beyond a single person to an organizational scale, the awkward, ugly in-between state becomes a universal pattern. That state of practice is referred to as hybrid.

In 2017, I served on the team that wrote and published the *Agile Practice Guide*,[12] a collaboration between the Project Management Institute and Agile Alliance. For the first time ever, both associations offered concrete guidance on hybrid approaches. Rather than divide the organization into bimodal's opposing mode 1 (predictive) and mode 2 (agile), it introduces four general patterns:

- **Pure agile, then pure predictive.** Designing a sky-scraper is a very iterative design effort. Many conversations lead to many sketches and models. But once we break ground, it becomes a very strict affair. Building the building is not, and should not be, as flexible as designing it was.
- **Combined agile and predictive.** For the annual release of the new smartphone model, we all know there's a lot of fancy graphics, sounds, and whiz-bang software that need an agile approach. However, during the whole year, there is a rather predictive supply chain project running in parallel, ensuring the thing can get built over and over.

- **Mostly predictive, with some agile.** A corporate training initiative will likely follow a pretty reliable life cycle, defined by the Association for Talent Development. We start with analysis of the needs, design, and develop the curriculum. Then we deliver the program to a pilot audience and iterate on the program with their feedback, after which we roll it out at scale.
- **Mostly agile, with some predictive.** Finally, we love our websites. Those are the most obvious agile projects, with lots of opinions on fonts, colors, text, and menus. Except for when it's time to move it into a predictively minded data center, who wants an infrastructure request well in advance.

Embracing the transitional hybrid reality reduces the burden to "get agility right." Moreover, many of these in-between combinations represent an approach that better aligns to the realities of a given product or service.

Bottom line? Don't ask "whether" agility. Ask "how much" agility. Don't ask whether a given project, department, or business unit should pursue agility. Instead, asking "how much" makes more sense.

Don't ask "whether" agility. Ask "how much" agility.

Say No to You in Everything

The lamentations of the average project manager usually sound like this:

As a project manager, I am the face of the project, which means I have to attend meetings with stakeholders and customers for most of the week, getting the fullest possible understanding of the goals and constraints we're working with. When I'm not in meetings, I check the specifications my team produces, because they often contain assumptions and vague statements that need to be clarified. Meanwhile, since I was assigned to this role based on my technical seniority, it's my responsibility to review the work items the team produces, which are generally okay, but not as good as they need to be. I stay late to correct whatever feedback my team gets from the compliance reports, which are often unfair and misdirected. Weekends are when I schedule all the meetings, catch up on emails, and type up reports. I'm working sixty hours a week, and I know I'm pulled in a lot of directions. But that's what it means to be a leader. Right?

The Afflictions

Sound familiar? This is the struggle with getting ahead in our careers: we gain more sphere of influence, more responsibility, more expectations. What was an exciting step forward becomes another and another, until it becomes exhausting, overwhelming, and painful. Here's how you got yourself into this.

Got Hero Syndrome?

Do you ever wish you could be cloned? There's so much work for you to do, and you're the best one to do that work. On the one hand, you're the thought leader that everyone comes to for decisions, perspectives, input, and expertise. On the other hand, you've become the bottleneck for both the organization's delivery and its growth.

This is often referred to as "hero syndrome." It's the belief that your value is based on being the center of gravity. If you don't do it, it won't get done right.

To scale your impact as a leader, you need to scale your capacity beyond your physical boundaries. This means leveraging more of your team. Which means shedding things that are beneath your role—less doing, more delegating. Which means investing more in building capacity in others to take on those tasks.

Got FOMO?

Have you noticed that you spend most of every day of every week in meetings? Don't worry, it's a common affliction. But what if I were to tell you that you didn't have to? If I were to challenge your involvement in so many things, what would your response be? Well, if you're honest with yourself, your response might sound like manager Maria:

But I have to go to those meetings! If I don't show up, then my peers are likely to change the direction without me weighing in. And if that happens, I have to clean it up. I'm out of the loop, and I'm not having the influence on decisions that I need to have. Moreover, a lot of the other leaders like to go to my team through back channels. And so I have to make sure that I'm aware of all the distractions that might be coming their way.

Finally, my boss likes being in the weeds and is asking for updates and details on everything going on, which means I have to go digging for that information, package it, and then brief him at the end of each day. It's just the culture here to be involved in both the decisions being made and the work being done.

Heck, that's what it means to be a leader, right?

Does this sound like someone you know?

This mindset is referred to as FOMO—fear of missing out. It's natural to want to be involved in as many things as possible. Knowledge is power, and the more knowledge leaders have, the better decisions they can make. Except we can't be everywhere. Moreover, the work we do today is becoming more and more complex, to the point where all the ins and outs simply can't fit into one person's mind. Just like with hero syndrome, you become the bottleneck.

The Prescription

Your teams need your support more than they need your output. You need an antidote. Here are some techniques to try to overcome your workload affliction.

The Personal Backlog

Maria has an overwhelming workload of transformation activities. She's held accountable for results, but several peers and stakeholders have opinions. So, like most good managers, she organizes it all into a sorted backlog like the one shown in the figure.

This is a simple technique that's been formalized countless times by countless books over the years. From the Franklin Plan-

Maria's Personal Backlog

1st Quarter Goals	Priority
Advanced agility course	High
Support Project X	High
Quarterly newsletter	Medium
Boot camp for Project Y	Medium
Charter Project Z	Low
Launch community of practice	Low

Maria
Manager

ner to Getting Things Done to the Bullet Journal, the principle is the same: effective self-leadership starts with "write it down."

It doesn't matter which personal productivity system you use, just use one. But it doesn't end there.

The Must/Want Filter

Yes, a personal backlog provides helpful clarity. But if you're an overachiever like me, failing to do the stuff on the lower end of the list is still very agitating. Missing the project Y boot camp makes me feel guilty, because the sponsor really wants me there. Missing the project X redo is frustrating, because I hate low-quality work. How do I move forward without the fear, uncertainty, and doubt that I'm going to be forever behind?

Several years ago I was wrestling with some family issues and sought out a family therapist to offer some perspective. He explained, "All of life's decisions can be boiled down into three emotional categories: Must Do's, Want To's, and Should Do's. And it's the Should Do's that are the source of all regret, pain, bitterness, and unfulfillment."

He went on to elaborate:

- **Must Do's** are the things that we choose to do because they align with a deeper definition, a larger vision of who we are as a human. We choose them, even if we don't want to, because we are compelled to. This is going to your brother's wedding even though that weekend is the same as a major work deadline.
- **Want To's** are the things that we choose to do because they fill us, energize us, and give joy. We choose them because we believe we are worth it, even if it means something else doesn't happen. This is going to the ball game with your friends Tuesday night, even if it means

that status report is a few hours late tomorrow after-
noon.

- **Should Do's** are the things that we submit to doing
  because we think we're supposed to. Not doing them
  would incur the disappointment of other people,
  making you feel guilty and embarrassed. These are
  things that are simultaneously annoying and unfulfill-
  ing. This is jumping on every phone call because that's
  what's expected of your role, even though you'll be
  catching up on email the whole time.

The distinction is between things we *choose* to do for personal
fulfillment or greater purpose versus the things we *submit* to
doing out of guilt or fear. The therapist further explained, "Anything on your list that you can't put into a Must Do or a Want
To is a Should Do that will suck your soul. Kill it. Remove it from
your list with the confidence of knowing it serves neither a greater
purpose nor a personal goal."

Therefore, Maria might rearrange that backlog to something
like the figure shown.

Maria's More Focused Backlog

Must do	← Should do →	Want to
Advanced agility course	~~Quarterly newsletter~~	Launch community of practice
Support Project X	~~Charter~~ ~~Project Z~~	
Train Project Y		

Maria
Manager

After some reflection, she realized her primary value right now is offering answers about new ways of working. That places a priority on training new pilots (Project Y) and staying a step ahead of everyone's maturity (advanced agility course). Meanwhile, the pressure to take over chartering is a Should Do, because that activity isn't impacted by the transformation yet. Moreover, updates will have to wait (quarterly newsletter) until there's something to report for successful pilots (Project X). Finally, Maria discovers in herself a need for peer support in order to stay strong under these pressures. That Community of Practice was originally just a good change management idea, but now feels like a deeper personal need.

This new list limits the change to the most critical items for right now. This feels right.

Offer a Crap Sandwich

Now that you've discovered your personal priorities and boundaries, it's time to enforce them in a way that gives credibility, rather than criticism.

One of the most helpful leadership tools I've come across is William Ury's "positive no."[13] In his book, he spells out a concrete process for saying no in a constructive, diplomatic fashion. Here's how it works:

1. **Say yes!** Acknowledge the value of the request.
2. **Say no.** Explain what you can't do and why, without apology.
3. **Say yes?** Offer meaningful alternatives to the request.

Let's see how team lead Ted turns a no into a positive, credibility-building response, when he's under a personal deadline.

Ted
Team Lead

"Hey, Ted, we need you to sneak in this layout change to the magazine issue, before it goes to print. We have a new advertiser with a long-term commitment, and they're eager to get some visibility right away."

- **Ted expresses his "yes!"** "Wow, that's awesome. Well done. Yes, I agree we need to get them set up with some impressions right away."
- **Ted asserts his "no."** "Unfortunately, the print layout specs are due today. Rearranging them will take at least two days, which would mean missing our print run."
- **Ted proposes his "yes?"** "The good news we have a ton of flexibility with the digital and social platforms. Since the sponsored content is going on the website, we could allocate some premium real estate there. Then we could simultaneously push a Facebook and Instagram campaign to boost it. Is that something you could work with?"

This follows a similar pattern for offering critical feedback sandwiched between two compliments. My wife refers to these patterns as the "love sandwich." I thought that was a great analogy until I shared it with a colleague named Steve who burst my bubble: "Actually, Jesse, that's not how it works. A chicken sandwich has chicken in the middle; a cheese sandwich has cheese in the middle. We label sandwiches by what's in the middle. So it's not a love sandwich you're offering. It's a crap sandwich."

So be it. To save my relationships, to be true to myself, to improve my performance in life, I offer the universe my crap sandwich. Just don't tell Ury that's what we're calling it.

Lonely Planet's New World

After some initial discovery, Luis started compiling a transformation backlog that looked very similar to those from his previous ventures.

- Restructure lines of reporting
- Refactor existing technical debt
- Overhaul employee compensation model
- Resolve the print-versus-digital issues
- Craft a new vision around the right market positioning
- Consolidate the diverse technology footprint
- Install modern innovation practices
- Find a new senior executive
- Install analytics to aid with product decisions
- Improve revenue strategy for existing digital products

And so on and so on. Like all of us in the change business, he was confronted with the question of where to begin. After talking through the options with the team, he settled on a strategy: do what we can while we wait for what we need.

Yes, the longer-term health of any organization comes from a clear, coherent vision, a true north. Yes, they needed a new senior executive. Yes, they needed to modernize the technology base. But all those things would take time to realize. Instead, there were other things that could be done right away. While those longer-term initiatives were being formulated, they started on several cleanup activities that would need to get done regardless of where the eventual vision would take them.

- The teams were formed into pods that featured product, engineering, and quality skill sets.

- Pods were formed around workstreams to address known gaps around analytics, search, and other technical debt.
- DevOps concepts like automated testing were prototyped on each of the pods.
- Meanwhile, research was started on the bigger-picture items.

The ownership was pleased to see a logical plan and some initial momentum. But the bigger organizational changes weren't happening fast enough for some of the senior staff, and they started complaining even more than before: "We've had such challenging leadership, how can we trust you? There's been so much change in the past, when do we get to the new org structure? How can we do good work before we solve the vision, the technology, the headcount?"

At this point, it would have been easy to be distracted by the criticisms of tenured managers who threatened to leave. Luis listened patiently to their emotions, but reiterated the strategy: "Yes, I agree these are challenges that need to be fixed. And we will get to them. But we'll focus first on the low-hanging fruit right now."

His stance kept most of the team on board, but not everyone. When the new digital product chief was selected from another department, two more resignations came in. In hindsight, everyone agrees that new leader was the right choice. But the baggage of the previous years was just too much for some people to carry through into yet another administration.

Luis held firm to transforming one small step at a time, and it started working. By the end of the following year, the new technology platform was in place. Agile team practices are the norm. Revenue is up. There is a breath of fresh air in the office. And Luis was even invited to accept a role as the president and CEO of the company.

Yes, it was painful. Yes, there were plenty of people unhappy with the transformation choices, and the pace of the transformation. But going slowly enabled more stability, and ensuring the cultural health of a decades-old company. That is no small feat. Luis's secret was focusing on less work at once. You can use the same secret. Overcome your workload by become a master of no.

Summary

In this chapter, we've explored the problem of workload. By exploiting every opportunity that comes our way, we've fallen behind on most of them. To regain our sanity, we've learned :

- **Say no to more delivery.** There will always be more work to do. Successful organizations make tough choices as to which projects deserve funding and how much. To get those done faster, you can build a systematic process of killing more of the lower priority projects.
- **Say no to more agility.** No, we should not go wholly agile/digital/lean overnight. Rather, strategic leaders assess where agility is needed the most and focus organizational resources there first.
- **Say no to yourself.** Our personal overcommitment stems from our perception of leadership as solving all the problems (hero syndrome) or participating in all conversations (fear of missing out). High-performing leaders take the time to run a mental audit on their personal backlog and make choices with intent.

It's time for you to switch from playing catch-up to playing in front. Doing that means mastering how to say no to everything slowing you down.

CHAPTER 6

Attack Culture
and Structure Together

Culture is like the wind. It is invisible, yet its effect can be
seen and felt.
—*Bryan Walker and Sarah A. Soule*

J anice already had enough to juggle; she didn't expect this.
 Reporting directly to the CIO for a large consulting company, Janice Brill was responsible for guiding her eighty-person
software organization through a much larger and broader transformation initiative worldwide. The IT group served a demanding army of consultants who made partner based on their ability
to generate results and revenue. As a result, the culture was one
that very much followed the chain of command and flow of value.
IT was a services organization serving a services organization.

So it was deeply gratifying to see the progress Janice and her management team made in the first few months of the formal change initiative. A transformation backlog was formed; a custom curriculum was developed to train and charter new pilot projects; they picked some promising team leads and had them kick off the first few pilots. Janice was feeling good.

Eventually, however, she started hearing more complaints and issues around one of the pilot projects. Since the team's direct people manager was fully focused on fighting another fire, she offered to check in on them to see what was going on.

The first team stand-up meeting was convened by Serena (not her real name), who served as the team facilitator. The meeting felt rather robotic. One by one, each person shared what they did yesterday, what they planned for the day, and whether they had any immediate blockers.

Meanwhile, Serena was logging blockers on an issues list that was multiple pages long. "Why are all these issues still open?" Janice asked. Serena seemed defensive and replied sheepishly, "Well, I've escalated each to the relevant partner in the firm, but I haven't heard anything back on most of them." Janice was surprised. Serena was a promising team lead, from whom she expected more follow-through. "Those partners are very busy. Have you tried following up?" The response was eye-opening: "Yes, I did. But the first few times, we got yelled at for wasting their time, even though the issues were directly impacting the projects they're sponsoring. I decided we should do our best to plow forward as is. It's just counterproductive to incur the drama."

Ouch. Despite using the new agile process consistently, the culture had snapped the organization back into its old habits. As a result, the pilot was in trouble, which means the transformation would take a credibility hit, and that would reflect on Janice's leadership. This was a problem.

Today's leaders are racing to reconfigure their organizations to be more adaptive and competitive. However, when looking for guidance on how to do just that, leaders will discover two competing schools of thought in the agile community: "First fix the culture" and "First fix the organizational structure." In reality, this debate between a culture-first and a structure-first strategy is a false choice.

The Problem with Philosophy

In this chapter, I reveal the pitfalls that have consumed too many would-be agility champions. They develop a strong, philosophically consistent approach to change, which somehow goes sideways.

- **The Boost.** Yes, it was good to use a consistent philosophy.
- **The Barrier.** And yet, they're reverting to old habits.
- **The Rebound.** So now, attack culture and structure together.

The Pattern of Untapped Philosophy

The Boost: Yes, It Was Good to Use a Consistent Philosophy

Janice knew she had a deeply entrenched culture. So she believed quickly getting results on the ground would be the best way to move the ball forward. And it did.

Leaders Use a Consistent Philosophy

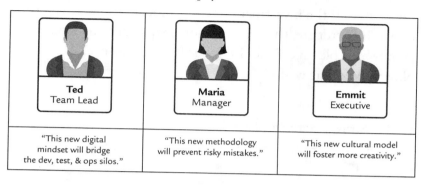

Ted Team Lead	**Maria** Manager	**Emmit** Executive
"This new digital mindset will bridge the dev, test, & ops silos."	"This new methodology will prevent risky mistakes."	"This new cultural model will foster more creativity."

Like Janice, maybe your agile strategy is focused on what we do. Any organization serves the purpose of creating results. So your transformation begins with installing popular practices for projects already in flight. You score quick wins to build momentum. You know it won't be perfect at first, so "fake it till we make it." Seeing is believing, so once they start getting results, people will buy in.

Or perhaps you're of the other school of thought, and believe agility is ultimately about who we are. It started with a so-called manifesto of values and principles.[1] Lean Startup is based on the entrepreneurial spirit of living in uncertainty. The whole idea of DevOps is to bridge the division between the development and operations departments. Therefore, you've crafted a strategy that involves executive listening tours, workshops about concepts and values, and regular communication of the vision of empowering staff to work differently.

The Barrier: And Yet, They're Reverting to Old Habits

Perhaps those new practices installed for quick wins generate immediate resistance. Or maybe the empowerment workshops and listening tours generated some initial energy, but people have gone back to their old habits. They say, "Oh, we believe in the transformation principles, but we have immediate deadlines to hit." After all the investment of time, money, and political capital to shift culture, the organization snaps back to its old ways. People have blown off the change as fluffy nonsense, and they've blown you off as well.

Leaders Struggle with Snapback

Ted Team Lead	**Maria** Manager	**Emmit** Executive
"Ugh. Why aren't people embracing the new mindset they agreed to?"	"Ugh. Why are so many people ignoring the methodology?"	"Ugh. Why have the culture workshops not impacted our policies?"

The Boost: So Now, Attack Culture and Structure Together

Culture is often described as "the way we do things around here." Naturally, that encapsulates both tangible things (policies, metrics, structures) and intangible things (values, symbols, language, behaviors, assumptions). The lines of reporting, defined roles, and career paths absolutely have impact on the vibe, the tone of daily life in an organization. And yet, the word "culture" is almost always used to describe the fuzzy elements of work, as if culture is separate and apart from those tangible elements. The truth is, structure and culture, the tangible and the intangible, are inextricably interconnected. You cannot evolve one without simultaneously impacting the other.

Change leaders can double their credibility with a strategy that incorporates both perspectives. In this chapter, we explore the following:

- **Overcome the culture-first trap.** How do we operationalize our desired culture in order to get momentum?
- **Overcome the structure-first trap.** How do we contextualize our new organizational structure in order to get staff on board?
- **The agile leadership canvas.** How you can use a collaborative brainstorming template to ensure you keep your balance and don't lean too far into one direction.

Through this two-sided conversation, we guide an organizational transition that is both meaningful and sustainable.

Despite several decades of success with agile methods, the debate still rages. What is the best way to get some quick wins? What is the best way to scale those wins across the organization? What is the best way to sustain those gains over the long haul? Since the beginning of the movement, the debate falls into two predictable camps.

The Two Schools of Transformation Approaches

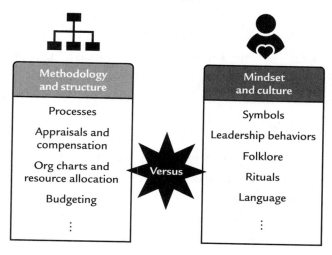

The first group will rightly say agile is a collection of approaches that reflect an underlying mindset. Any change we make in our organizations can only be sustained by the right cultural mindset. We must change our culture first.

Others will recommend changing structure first. These experts will highlight that culture is amorphous and nebulous. It is more achievable to start with adjustments to policy, org structure, role definitions, and other such tangible items. Culture, as it turns out, comes last.

In truth, the reality is this is the classic trap of a false choice. The most successful transitions to organizational agility feature a simultaneous blending of both cultural shifts and structural changes. Unfortunately, too many change champions fall prey to one of these camps. Let's take a look at how easy it is to fall into these transformation pitfalls.

The Culture-First Trap

Here's a typical story I've heard from several champions of agility, as told from Ted's perspective.

Ted
Team Lead

Ted attends an agile conference. In one presentation, he hears, "Agility is a mindset. It means shifting from a fixed mindset to a growth mindset." In another session, he hears, "DevOps is not about tools, it's about culture. Unless you fix the underlying belief systems of the organization, people will not perform the practices."

Ted learns that merely "doing Scrum/Lean Startup/DevOps" doesn't create lasting change. You need to change who you are as a team. He decides this is what he wants his team to be about. When he returns to the office, he declares at the next meeting, "As of today, we are an agile team. We are going to be an oasis of awesome. The one team that shows everyone what excellence looks like." He prints and hands out business cards to everyone on the team with those values printed on them, believing in his bones this will inspire new behaviors.

The rest of the team, including the manager, are dumbfounded. During lunch, many joke quietly, "I wonder what kind of drugs they were handing out at that conference?" "Let's see how long it takes for this to pass by."

A week later, the team is locked in a very loud argument.

"What on earth are you doing to all the reports, Bob?"

"Well, Ted says we're empowered now, so I changed the layout for all the RMT reports, because they were just wrong."

Ted is stunned and chimes in. "What?! Empowerment is one thing, but you've got to let people know what you're doing."

Bob is confused. "But Tisha has been working on her thing without any status. I'm not doing anything different than her."

Tisha confirms the story, barely blinking as she says, "Yep. Given that we're experimenting now, I've been using a prototype design process. I decided that was more important than the support tickets we usually do."

Because Ted wants to be consistent with the cultural philosophy, he resists the demands to dictate any new behaviors or policies. That blowup becomes the first in a series of disagreements on what the new values actually mean. Six weeks later, the team is in bitter disarray, and Ted is ready to throw in the towel.

Many of the unicorn organizations we admire in business today feel fundamentally different from our own. They use funny jargon. Every day is casual Friday. Managers are nowhere to be found, and custom art is hanging in the halls. Because they feel different, they attract and retain better talent, and they are more comfortable taking innovative risks.

Simply put, successful organizations have vastly different cultures than average organizations. It's a truism that we take for granted. Which is why the culture-first approach resonates so deeply in modern business. "Culture comes from the top," as the saying goes. But when you start there, and stay there, you run into two very painful realities.

Pitfall: All Sizzle, No Steak

Most experts will agree a common theme across the agile/digital/lean movements is that each is primarily about a new mindset. Leaders and teams are challenged to let go of their decades of training and experience in favor of a new way of working. It's much more important to emphasize "being agile" than merely "doing agile."

My university literature professor once explained to me that "You can't speak to the general without the specific. You can't talk about grief until you tell the story of a recent widower unconsciously walking the streets to his wife's favorite coffee shop at midnight in the rain."

Likewise, talking about noble virtues like honesty, respect, and value sounds great. But until you hang something tangible on those values, they aren't visible. Until the invisible is made visible, change simply will not happen. People will ask, "What do I do differently? Is my job at risk? What does that look like? Where do I start?"

Even more unsettling is that you run the risk of losing credibility in your role. One organization I worked with had to shift one manager to a new role. When describing the challenge, his vice president explained it to me like this, "He's a great person, but he only talks a great game and never does anything. When his team comes to him asking for guidance and direction, he simply tells them, 'You're empowered—go figure it out.' That group has been stuck for a while, because he's not adding the substance they're asking for. He's all sizzle, no steak. All hat, no cattle."

Pitfall: Your Agile Is Not My Agile

When leaders live in abstraction, followers are left to interpretation. Simply issuing the order "go forth and collaborate" will result in very different kinds of collaboration across the organization. Humans need details. Unless we offer concrete examples or guidelines, they will not thrive with mere platitudes.

Just as the old parenting adage goes, there is freedom in boundaries. People thrive knowing what is safe harbor and what is out of bounds. Without something explicit in the way of universal guidelines, your teams will argue over what agile means. Tragically, if they are all different, they'll all be justified in their positions, drifting even farther apart, leading to more conflict, more delays, and more execution issues.

Ted isn't the only one. Zappos CEO Tony Hsieh has famously been pushing the edge of self-organization at the online retailer. In 2014, he installed the Holacracy method, to encourage a culture of self-organized employees making faster decisions with more engagement. At the time, it was heralded as the most progressive management experiment in the tech industry. But that experiment started with the assumption that managers were no longer needed and staff could do whatever they wanted. That created a Wild West dynamic that took time to corral and settle. Years later, Zappos is very proud of the unique dynamic they have, but let's be honest. Most other organizations simply do not have the stomach for that bumpy of a journey, regardless of how golden the destination.[2]

The Structure-First Trap

Now that we know a culture-first approach isn't ideal, it's easy to see the appeal of making big structural changes. Here's how that scenario generally goes.

Emmit
Executive

Emmit attends a certification workshop that details the ROCKIN agility method. He becomes convinced it is the ideal strategy for the organization to transition to a faster, better, cheaper version of itself.

To accelerate the transformation, he hires one of the "big five" consulting firms to help make it happen. The ROCKIN consultants descend upon the organization, wielding their templates, org charts, and flow charts. People are allocated to new "innovation pods" and informed that their new roles will be totally different. New, unfamiliar project management tools are installed, and "coaches" hover over people, instructing them in the new way to do their new jobs.

Because these changes are made so swiftly, staff feel confused and begin to slow down out of fear of making mistakes. Meanwhile, middle management feels isolated by the role shifting, so they begin actively resisting the initiative.

Within a year, Ted becomes frustrated with the consistent push-back and the pain-to-reward ratio, fires the consultancy, and the initiative is dialed back. The new processes are diluted into something that looks more familiar but has limited impact. Finally, the most forward-thinking champions declare, "That's not agile," and leave the firm to become consultants themselves.

At first glance, this structure-first approach has advantages over Ted's culture-first philosophy. Namely, we can actually see that something different actually happened. There are material changes on the ground. However, without a direct effort to incorporate cultural elements, two recurring pitfalls emerge.

Pitfall: Too Fast, Too Furious

Several agility pioneers believe strongly in this approach. Craig Larman, the cocreator of the Large Scale Scrum (LeSS) method, starts all of his consulting engagements with a staff restructure.[3] Author Jeff Sutherland has popularized another all-or-nothing approach known as "shock therapy."[4]

However, that barrier to entry is simply too high for regular people. This approach requires a significantly high pain tolerance on the part of everyone from team leads to senior leaders. Often, it requires a willingness (even an eagerness) to incur conflict within your leadership team, turnover of your most tenured people, and even the risk of litigation from those who feel betrayed.

Granted, change of any kind is unsettling to some. But by definition, those leaders who advance change have a higher change tolerance than the mean average of the people inside the organization. Moreover, you may be willing to disrupt your own department, but then how will those changes impact your customers, vendors, and partners.? You may want to be agile, but is everyone else on board? Most of your stakeholders will share your frustration with known problems but will be unwilling to help fix them.

Move too fast, and you might leave behind the people you wanted to follow you in the first place.

Pitfall: Action Without Intent Is Noise

Even if you take a measured pace, your staff and stakeholders will still be asking you, "Why?" There is a reason why the most compelling organizations have mission statements. They create clarity and focus. By articulating a vision of what we are trying to achieve, and why we even want to achieve it, people are able to place action within a context.

In a *Harvard Business Review* article, Boris Groysberg and Michael Slind summarize this dynamic, explaining leadership as a conversation. Gone are the days where universal, one-size-fits-all edicts pass muster. From technology to globalization to upcoming generations, several business trends are "forcing the shift from corporate communication to organizational conversation."[5] Modern leadership is about conversations.

Modern leadership is about conversations.

Even more common, impatient leaders will often jump to a structural fix before a proper root cause analysis determines the underlying problem at hand. The quick fix yields little results, so another new silver bullet method is implemented, and so on, and so on. Facilitating real conversation enables true reflection. Without that, you run the risk of several successive knee-jerk mandates, each of which inspires change fatigue and lowers morale.

The False Choice of Transformation Philosophy

	Culture-First	Structure-First
Belief System	Agility is a mindset. Your transformation will only be skin-deep until you change hearts and minds.	Agility is about results. Your transformation won't make headway until you make serious changes.
Theory of Change	Beliefs drive behaviors. Culture is the proven primary barrier to agility. Being agile is better than merely doing agile.	Culture comes last. Fake it till you make it. Seeing is believing.
Pros	• Addresses underlying psychology that drives behavior • Sets an aspirational vision of where the organization is going	• Clarifies change into actionable tasks • Sets firm boundaries and expectations for new behaviors
Cons	• Makes the change vague and open to interpretation • Most are left wondering "What do I do differently, exactly?"	• Degree of change is too much for the current culture • Many are left wondering "Why are we even changing in the first place?"

A Holistic Philosophy

As you can see, a one-sided perspective on leading agile organizations can spell trouble. However, each perspective brings necessary truths to the table, as we can see in the figure.

Instead of falling into this classic trap, the most effective leaders capture the best of both worlds in a blended approach. Here are three tips and a case study that reveal how to do just that.

Tip: Operationalize the Culture

In order to ground a culture-oriented thought process, we want to reshape it with some structural elements. To do that, we simply ask one question: "How do we operationalize this?"

If you're locked in a conversation about the pain of today versus the promise of tomorrow, you can ground that conversation with this simple prompt. Rather than wandering along in a fog of vague values, explore a tangible, visible, physical change that can move the status quo.

A Holistic Approach to Transformation

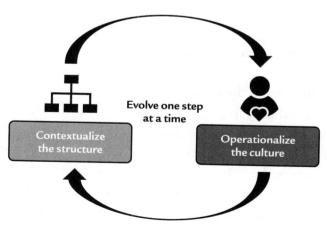

Evolve one step
at a time

Contextualize
the structure

Operationalize
the culture

In her best-selling book *Dare to Lead*, research professor Brené Brown talks about the uselessness of talk without action:

> If you're not going to take the time to translate values from ideals to behaviors—if you're not going to teach people the skills they need to show up in a way that's aligned with those values and then create a culture in which you hold one another accountable for staying aligned with the values—it's better not to profess any values at all. They become a joke. A cat poster. Total BS.[6]

Instead, she offers an elegant way to turn beliefs into behaviors. For each value you aspire to emulate, discuss these three questions:

- What are three behaviors that support this value?
- What are three slippery behaviors that are outside this value?
- What's an example of a time when you were fully living into this value?

It's that simple—and that powerful.

Tip: Contextualize the Structure

Meanwhile, the more analytical leaders on your senior team will want to go straight to mechanics. That's good. But to inform those changes as more than just management mandate, ask the opposing question: "How do we contextualize this?"

For every new process or policy, challenge yourself with "why." "Why do we need to change at all? What's the real problem here?" Then be prepared to broadcast those answers, over and over and over again.

In the best-selling book *Power of Habit*, Charles Duhigg explains the neurology of change.[7] The basal ganglia is where we process routine, standard operating procedures. The prefrontal cortex is where we force ourselves to try something different. There is literally a different part of the brain involved in day-to-day activities versus new behaviors.

That means we need a lot of encouragement and repetition to replace old habits with new ones. Leaders can help that by repeating the context of the change, over and over again.

Tip: Transformation via Evolution

Transformation is all the rage. Every new executive wants to be the turnaround leader who made a mark and left a legacy in record time. But beware, hotshot. If you go too fast and too furious, you might just wipe out.

In his book *Adapt*, Tim Harford explains that the modern toaster is so complex, no one person is able to build one independently.[8] Consider integrating a heating element, a voltage transformer, a heat-resistance shelf, a spring-action ejector, and a rotary timer. That did not happen overnight; it is the culmination of decades of gradual adjustments and enhancements interjected by one manufacturer and then another.

Building a new team, let alone a new organization, is way more complex than a toaster. It requires both a great deal of energy and a great deal of time. This means we are faced with the fundamental tension: sustainable change requires that we be impatient with the status quo but patient with the people in it.

The agile leader's dilemma: Be impatient with the status quo but patient with the people in it.

To add insult to injury, the larger the organization, the more likely change is needed, and also the more step-wise your agile journey should be. Let's hear how one leadership team was able to pull it off.

Case Study: United States Government Program

Several years ago, the human resources office of the United States federal government was reeling from unfulfilled initiatives. In response, then-director of the Office of Personnel Management, John Berry, declared a new strategy: "After failing three times to modernize the federal retirement system with the big bang approach, the Office of Personnel Management is taking a new tack that focuses on incremental changes."[9] He set a new cultural tone.

Deep inside the organization, one branch chief heard the message. The leadership team for the USA Staffing program took the challenge to heart. In 2012, they embraced agile methods as a way to realize Berry's new vision within their own program, which is a key service in hiring government employees.[10] First, they operationalized the new methods for only a single delivery team, keeping true to the direction of "one step at a time." Then the next step was to build a program-wide competency in product ownership with role definitions and training. These were immediate structural changes.

During this phase, they made an important cultural discovery: attracting the right change-minded people was more critical than where those people were stationed. So they adjusted their remote work policies and expanded their internal recruitment beyond the Washington, D.C., area.

With a strong team in place, they were then able to parse the agile value of partnering by hosting recurring focus group meetings. These meetings continue to this day, allowing partners and stakeholders to share frustrations and ideas in an open forum. It worked. They've been able to modernize their program and build customer confidence through an evolution of both the tangible and intangible aspects of organizational design.

Their strategy was based on a holistic philosophy. First, Berry set a cultural tone by issuing the mandate, "What we've been doing isn't working. We are doing things differently. Period." Right after the cultural message, one branch chief responded with several structural changes: pilot projects, competency development, role definitions. Then the remote policy and the focus groups turned cultural values into tangible, tactical actions.

This yin-yang approach created sustainable change. The good news is it's not magic. It's repeatable. You can do this too, using a simple template.

The Agile Leadership Canvas

It can be challenging to strike the right blend of institutional and inspirational change. As a result, executives will be tempted to hire consultants to install a proprietary commercial methodology detached from your context. However, it turns out to be a rather simple proposition. To help that conversation, we are fans of the Agile Leadership Canvas™. Here's how it works.

Canvas Design

The Agile Manifesto is the foundational document that chartered the agile movement. It advocates four complementary values to achieve better business outcomes:

- **Empowering:** Individuals and interactions over processes and tools
- **Delivering:** Working product over comprehensive documentation

- **Partnering:** Customer collaboration over contract negotiation
- **Adapting:** Responding to change over following a plan

Our collective goal is to create organizations that emulate these values and generate those outcomes again and again, year after year. When we superimpose these values on the two-sided conversation of agile culture and agile structure, we create a simple grid that can be used to elicit and compare ideas for evolving the organization.

Agile Leadership Canvas

| | Culture
Symbols, rituals, folklore, language, leadership behaviors | Structure
Processes, policies, people allocation, budgets, appraisals, reporting |
|---|---|---|
| **Empowering**
We value individuals and interactions over processes and tools | "The unicorn trophy goes to this month's person with the craziest idea that actually worked." | "Staff have several ideas for the new facility. Let's increase our investment to make some of them happen." |
| **Delivering**
We value working product over comprehensive documentation | "Let's get a prototype into limited release this quarter. We'll declare victory and use the results to plan a second phase." | "Our most strategic projects have 100% allocated staff. We don't want anything else distracting them." |
| **Partnering**
We value customer collaboration over contract negotiation | "Remember that time we walked away from a $1M deal because our teaming partner was getting shut out ..." | "Let's add a clause in the agreement that preserves your executive discretion to make changes within certain parameters." |
| **Adapting**
We value responding to change over following a plan | "YES! We can totally rework that deliverable. It's annoying, but now we know a better way." | "Every month let's hold a public stakeholder feedback review. Any new ideas or changes will be formally prioritized against existing goals." |

Maria Uses the Canvas Holistically

Maria
Manager

Let's see how manager Maria could use the canvas to guide her team toward a holistic change strategy.

After several weeks of research on how to bring agility into her department, Maria believes it's time to make her move. She calls her team together and says, "You know I've been investigating how agility could drive our group to better results. I think it's time to start moving forward, but I need your help to figure out how."

She hands out the canvas and asks, "Which of these values resonate with you? Which of these will move the needle forward?"

Some people begin brainstorming on empowerment. Web developer Divya says, "I do think we could benefit from a more empowered workforce. That will help us attract and retain talent, which we seem to be having a hard time doing."

Maria presses further: "What would that look like operationally?"

Divya replies, "I liked that article you shared about Amazon being among the most remote-friendly workplaces.[11] Perhaps we could announce a new work-from-home experiment."

Lead analyst Larry responds, "That's a good idea. Meanwhile, I'm thinking that we encourage a shift toward empowerment by making things fun. I liked that post about Tata Group's annual Failure Award to encourage daring innovation."[12]

These first ideas are recorded onto the canvas.

Later in the conversation, Orlando, the operations person, speaks up, "I'm frustrated with failed projects. This is the core value that resonates with me the most. I say we need to mandate collaboration, where nobody works from home, and create more accountability around any mistakes. There's just not enough discipline here."

Agile Leadership Canvas

	Culture *Symbols, rituals, folklore, language, leadership behaviors*	Structure *Processes, policies, people allocation, budgets, appraisals, reporting*
Empowering *We value individuals and interactions over processes and tools*	WORK–FROM–HOME "FAILURE AWARD"	
Delivering *We value working product over comprehensive documentation*		
Partnering *We value customer collaboration over contract negotiation*		
Adapting *We value responding to change over following a plan*		

Maria knows they've hit on a key conflict. "That's a good point, Orlando. But that goes directly against the other ideas we had. Perhaps we could have both an empowering and delivering organization. What might that look like?"

Wanting to keep things positive, Divya chimes in, "What if our work-from-home policy is reserved for our rock stars? We set the precedent that it's an earned privilege and an incentive for high-value candidates."

Orlando responds to her intent, "Okay, I see where you're going. From our audit last year, we found that quality issues were the top cause of project delays and complaints. I've been wanting to encourage more ownership of those gaps. So instead of only doing the HR-mandated training path, what if we take personal

Agile Leadership Canvas

	Culture *Symbols, rituals, folklore, language, leadership behaviors*	Structure *Processes, policies, people allocation, budgets, appraisals, reporting*
Empowering *We value individuals and interactions over processes and tools*	WORK-FROM-HOME "FAILURE AWARD"	FORMALIZE IT AS INCENTIVE. ONLY FOR ROCK STARS
Delivering *We value working product over comprehensive documentation*	ADMIT OUR QUALITY PROBLEM	$2K PROFESSIONS DEV. BUDGET FOR RELATED TOPICS
Partnering *We value customer collaboration over contract negotiation*		
Adapting *We value responding to change over following a plan*		

ownership of how to use our annual professional development budget? It could be spent on any work-related training that addresses our top team priorities."

Excited at the new level of creativity, the team jots down those revisions.

Eventually, Larry interjects, "Team, this was a good conversation, but honestly, I think trying these ideas will be plenty for now. If we do more than this, our people will freak out. Let's try this for a couple months, and see if we generate movement."

Janice Takes a Stand

After confirming that the cultural problem was more than an outlier, Janice Brill made a decision. With all the progress made on installing new team structures, new processes, and new tools, it was time to make a cultural statement.

Pulling the Scrum Master aside, Janice offered the truth and some support. "I am sure you have noticed the team is not resolving open issues, deliverables are slipping, and stakeholders are getting grumpy. If it's okay with you, I would like to step in temporarily and show you a different way of engaging the team and the stakeholders."

Over the next two weeks, Janice formally inserted herself into the team and started using much more of an assertive style. When the team started sharing their daily updates as if reporting status to her, she would snap, "Don't talk to me—these are your teammates. You tell them what you need."

Later, she walked Serena over to one of the principal partners and said, "Hey, Bob, I hear you've been sitting on an either-or decision on which data policy you want us to follow for the data modernization project. So which is it?" The partner barked back, "Hey, Janice, you know I'm busy. I haven't had the time to look at the pros and cons." Janice bit back, "Fair enough, then does that mean Serena gets to decide for you? If we don't make a decision now, we lose two weeks on the deadline, which is how long you've had this question." "Fine. Just use the EU policy for now. That one's the tightest, so it will cover most cases. We good?"

Janice smiled. "Yes, we are. Thank you." As they walked into the elevator, Janice turned to Serena and said, "This is what empowerment looks like, Serena. There is a time for coaching, and there is a time for leading. You should be showing your team members how you stand up for what needs to be done."

That lesson was meant for her, but it also serves as a lesson for us. Sometimes encouraging our staff is not enough. In order to cement our structural changes, we need to make the cultural statement of role modeling the behavior we want to see.

"There is a time for coaching, and there is a time for leading." — Janice Brill

Summary

In this chapter, we confronted the debate between "doing agile" and "being agile." By trying to be philosophically consistent, we've learned about:

- **The culture-first trap.** This leads to the charge that your change is "all sizzle, no steak." Moreover, it leaves the transformation open to uncontrolled variation and interpretation.
- **The structure-first trap.** Here you run the risk of going too fast, too furious. Moreover, without sufficient context, your staff will view the change as noise.
- **The agile leadership canvas.** We can use a collaborative brainstorming template to align our teams on how to attack culture and structure in a holistic fashion.

It is a fact that how we approach change is often driven by our philosophy. Unfortunately, too much of the conversation around organizational agility is limited to all-or-nothing approaches. A project is either agile or traditional. We use either this methodology or that one. A transformation is either culture-driven or structure-driven.

The best leaders are those who can move beyond these false choices and spark a simple conversation around both sides of the equation.

CHAPTER 7

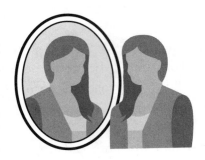

Look in the Mirror

What got you here will not get you there.
—*Marshall Goldsmith*

Brian was not expecting his agile journey to hit an inflection point, but it did in 2017.

For more than ten years, Brian Hackerson had been serving as a laboratory manager at an R&D lab for a global conglomerate making products that ranged from battery parts to automobile lubricants to home decorations. During his tenure the lab served mostly as an internal job shop. A product manager would ask him for an engineer, he would find the right skill set, log the charge code, and move on to the next request.

His office was also progressing with the times. He'd read the hot books like *Lean Startup* and saw a need for speed and innovation. They even took a trip to Silicon Valley and visited companies like Uber to see firsthand what modern practices look like. Given the R&D lab was inside a much larger organization, they would incorporate whatever new technique was doable within their sphere of operation. They were a stable, reliable contributor to new products.

Then 2017 happened. New leadership was installed at the CTO office and with it a new mandate: "We want you to shift from responding to R&D requests to driving innovation. Go figure out how we're going to create value out of these modern software technologies around the cloud, mobility, big data, AI, and so on."

Full of inspiration and support, Brian started making changes. He organized teams of three or four to work as a team figuring out what idea to deliver in a given month and start showing to people. Given the company's culture was very socially networked, it wasn't a complete surprise that people started talking. Word got around, more and more people got curious. Momentum was building.

A new boss and a new mandate were change enough. But then shortly after that announcement, a different set of leaders arranged for Jeff Sutherland, cocreator of the Scrum framework, to come to the corporate campus and teach a two-day workshop on product innovation. The coincidence was too much to pass up. Brian took the hint from the greater forces of fate, went to the workshop, and was summarily blown away. He describes it this way:

> I was struck by his passion for what he was doing. Here's a guy in his seventies saying, "I'm here to save the world from soul-sucking work." And I was just like, "Yes, yes please. More of that." I've been leading an R&D function for years, so these concepts weren't foreign or brand new to me. But I came to appreciate, working with Jeff, the need for good technique and the power of purpose. So because of that, I self-selected into this role as the

transformation leader and said, "There are other people that are probably far more qualified on paper, but I know this organization, I know the company. I can make this happen." And so I went after it.[1]

What had been a set of informal experiments was now a formal role, and it began to snowball. More and more people were coming to visit the lab, ask questions, and request help. Fast-forward a year into the journey, and the total number of visitors hit a thousand.

This was getting big. Fast.

Eventually, the pressure started mounting. Brian began to feel burnout and to wonder about his own performance as a leader: What if I don't have all the answers? What if I can't get to everyone who wants help? What if we start making mistakes? It soon became overwhelming.

In reality, he was doing just fine. But his own self-perception of his performance was becoming an issue.

What happened is actually more fundamental. It was what was going on between my own ears. The imposter had moved in, taken up residence, and was running not just my day job but running my life.

The transformation had hit an unexpected, personal roadblock.

The Problem with Leadership

As discussed earlier in this book, a key aspect of fostering organizational agility is the evolution of the organization's cultural mindset. Therefore, as a change leaders we tend to be externally focused on shepherding the mindset change in the people around us: senior leaders, peers, teams. But there's one person whose growth we tend to forget about: ourselves.

In case you haven't noticed, the underlying thread so far in this book is *you*. Whether you are like Brian and initiated your role of agile leader, or you were ordered to take the task of creating agility in the organization, you are the originator of the next phase. As the champion for improving the way we work, you are the fulcrum, you are the force multiplier.

You are the agile leader.

Serving this role will ask much of you. It will require

... more of your effort than you think,

... more depth than you already have, and therefore

... more personal change than you could ever anticipate.

In Brian's story, he had been on a gradual and steady move toward modern practices. He already had an agile mindset. But when it came to emulating, broadcasting, and reproducing that mindset at a larger scale, he simply was not fully prepared for the ride.

For other leaders, the struggle is the other way around: you see what needs to happen, but your staff, your peers, your leadership team simply aren't changing as meaningfully or as quickly as needed. You feel dragged down by the very organization you are trying to change, and it's just exhausting.

The personal leadership journey for any agile champion is almost always the most forgotten element of the transformation and simultaneously the most important.

Here's how the transformation happens on a personal level:

- **The Boost.** Yes, it was good to mobilize them toward real change.

- **The Barrier.** And yet, the pace and degree of change feel wrong.
- **The Rebound.** So now, look in the mirror.

The Pattern of Untapped Leadership

The Boost: Yes, It Was Good to Mobilize Them Toward Real Change

You introduced new techniques. People are experimenting. New conversations are happening. Both resistance and results are emerging.

Leaders Mobilize Their People

Ted Team Lead	Maria Manager	Emmit Executive
"We should use these design patterns for our digital deliverables."	"We can run a pilot to see if this approach works for us."	"We are going to 90% agile by end of the year."

The Barrier: And Yet, the Pace and Degree of Change Feel Wrong

People are doing it wrong. Skeptics are fighting back. Too many are reverting to old habits. Others are taking credit and taking control. Everyone is pulling in all directions. This is not what you bargained for.

Leaders Struggle with the Change They Created

Ted Team Lead	Maria Manager	Emmit Executive
"Ugh. People are using these patterns inconsistently."	"Ugh. Other departments are starting their own pilots."	"Ugh. No matter how much we change, we're still not good enough."

The Rebound: So Now, Look in the Mirror

Can you tolerate agile mistakes? Can you accept leadership expectations different from yours? You forgot about changing yourself.

In order to scale the leadership capacity of the organization, we have to start with the key role model for those behaviors. We have to start with you.

In this chapter, we will explore the ways in which an agile journey will put your personal leadership to the ultimate test:

- **The leadership gap.** We will explore the unique expectations placed upon leaders in today's context, and the very real pattern that most leaders do not live up to those expectations.
- **Defining effective leadership.** Research has proven the specific leadership competencies required to thrive in such environments.
- **Close the gap.** Finally, we will talk about two key practices shown to build leadership capacities to achieve higher levels of impact: consistent reflection and intentional feedback.

Agile organizations are only created by those leaders who exhibit personal agility. If you're curious about what the next level looks like, then let's explore exactly what that means.

The Leadership Gap

Over and over, we hear about the problem with senior leadership. In our survey research, we see a recurring barrier to organizational agility:[2]

"Inadequate management support and sponsorship"
"Lack of agile executive leadership"
"Lack of support from executive leadership"
"No sponsorship/support from senior management"

The temptation is to think that this refers exclusively to executives. Certainly that is important. Change management research confirms the greatest indicator of successful change is "visible and active sponsorship." However, that same body of research also asserts that our people want to hear how their specific job is impacted "from their direct supervisor."[3] That means our teams need clear engagement from the top-level leader to the lowest-level leader, and therefore everyone in between.

If you are an influencer, then you are the leader they are looking to. Also, if you are leading an organization into a new way of working, then by definition, others are following *behind* you. You are farther in your journey than most of the people you are mobilizing. They need you to scale your leadership capacity, so that you are able to

- Tolerate those who are slow to adopt
- Show empathy to those who resist and complain
- Explain the changes and the reasons for them

- Frame the changes in the context of where your teams have been before
- Adjust your talking points, depending on your audience

In their book *Scaling Leadership*, Robert Anderson and William Adams, the creators of the Leadership Circle, describe this tension as a gap between the leadership you are capable of and the leadership that is needed of you. Specifically, "The complexity of my heart and mind, my internal operating system, is not enough for the complexity of the context we face."[4]

Most of us have learned our leadership roles in a different context. We're used to the stability, certain simplicity, and clarity of what we know. We're used to this. But the world is moving into a more challenging reality, often referred to as a VUCA world. VUCA is a term coined by Warren Bennis and Burt Nanus in the 1980s, and popularized by the U.S. military over the last several years. It describes the nature of today's world that makes leadership so hard:

- **Volatility** is unexpected change, causing disruption. What was true yesterday is no longer true, throwing everything into disarray.
- **Uncertainty** is unknown change expected in advance, causing anxiety. This is knowing that whichever road you take could be the wrong one.
- **Complexity** is unexpected scale and interdependency, causing overwhelmedness. As soon as you're confident of a path forward, more information comes to light.
- **Ambiguity** is about unwanted ownership, causing frustration. With so much happening so fast, we have to move forward with imperfect information. This forces our people to make more detailed assumptions than they are unaccustomed to making.

And so many of us—whether we're a team lead, middle manager, or executive—we're still expecting stability, certainty, simplicity, and clarity. But we've watched the world change right in front of us, and everyone in our teams, departments, and organizations are looking to us for how to move forward. That's the leadership gap. Put another way, an organization's agility cannot exceed the agility of its leaders. Your leadership skills and tool kit are being stretched like never before. You need to fill this gap.

An organization's agility cannot exceed the agility of its leaders.

Defining Effective Leadership

Since the dawn of mankind, the debate has raged over what constitutes good leadership. From generals to monarchs to priests, humanity has assessed leadership prowess against a smorgasbord of characteristics. Even through the industrial era and into the twentieth century, good leaders were said to be more extroverted, more charismatic, more masculine, more intelligent, and just better overall human beings. This culminated in the Great Man theory, popularized by Thomas Carlyle in the mid-nineteenth century, who concluded "The history of the world is but the biography of great men."[5]

In other words, the beginnings of modern management included the notion that effective leaders are supposedly born and not made. The bad news is this mindset carried on from generation to generation, in every field of leadership. The good news is that simply does not match with science. We now live in a world that benefits from the very real research into what leadership means, what works and what does not work, who can and who cannot thrive.

Let's take a look.

Effective Leadership Is Flexible, Not Fixed

Without question, the most popular leadership model over the last several decades is situational leadership.[6] Its key point is that as followers journey through varying degrees of competence and confidence, the leader should apply an appropriate amount of support or direction. Effective leadership, therefore, is not about the most powerful *innate* style, but about the most *appropriate* style.

There is a sort of common sense to the concept: be the leader a given person needs you to be. As a supporting point, all of us have been unimpressed by that grumpy supervisor who would declare, "My leadership style is my style. If people can't handle it, that's on them." Unfortunately, those grumpy supervisors are butting up against a leadership principle that has been formalized over the better part of a century:

- Published in 1975, the Path-Goal Theory asserts that a specific leadership style is only effective based on the employee's goals and the nature of the work at hand.[7]
- From 1967, the Fielder contingency model states that a leader's effectiveness is based on two variables: leadership style and situational favorableness.[8]
- Starting in 1939, the Harwood studies by Kurt Lewin were the first to formulate distinct leadership styles, and found that each had a different kind of impact on the culture of a study group.[9] These studies became the foundation of the field of organizational development.

The most popular validation of the idea of context-driven leadership came in a landmark article in 2000 by the sometimes controversial author of *Emotional Intelligence*, Daniel Goleman. The article published a study measuring the correlative impact between specific leadership style and organizational impact. The conclusion?

The best leaders don't know just one style of leadership—they're skilled at several, and have the flexibility to switch between styles as the circumstances dictate.[10]

As champions of modern ways of working, this means your people need you to exhibit personal agility. Not merely to role model the adaptiveness to change we're promoting but also to have the patience, empathy, and humility to guide them in their walk.

Effective Leadership Is Balanced, Not Biased

Many debates over effective influence center around whether leaders should focus on people skills or achievement skills—whether it is relationships that drive results or action. The science tell us sustainable impact requires both.

Let's go back to Anderson and Adams. Their research has yielded what they describe as the Universal Model for Leadership,[11] and rests on a body of over 1 million data points. The data reveals that effective leadership correlates to effectively wielding both the people side and the task side of the proverbial coin.

The People Side of Leadership

On the one side, effective leaders create new possibilities through relational competencies like *caring connection, collaborator, composure,* among others. In contrast to the Great Man theory, the research shows that these competencies are only effective when performed with purpose and intent. Moreover, these skills improve with practice over time.

By contrast, when those relational skills are overrun by impulse and instinct, they turn into counterproductive reactions like *pleasing, passive,* and *distant.* Put another way, when a leader is too focused on the people side, it can negatively impact results and thus effectiveness.

The Task Side of Leadership

On the other side of the leadership conversation are task-oriented competencies like *sustainable productivity, systems thinking,* or *purpose and vision.* Similarly, when these skills are over-applied or done merely on reactive instinct, they too have a darker side that cloud the leader as *perfectionist, autocratic,* and *arrogant.*

Bill Joiner, a Boston area researcher, has been collecting his own data on leaders worldwide. His findings point to a progression of sequential stages of increasing leadership skill. One compelling discovery is how power is displayed at each increasing skill level.[12]

At the most common skill level (45 percent of all managers), leaders are overly assertive with subordinates and overly accommodative to their supervisor. These are two distinct power styles that exist in every leader. But at lower skill levels, they show up at distinctly different scenarios, based mostly on instinct and reaction. However, as leaders grow, increasing their depth and capacity, Joiner noticed an increasing blend of these two power stances: more listening to our people and speaking truth more often to those in higher positions. The highest levels of leadership performance show a near seamless interweaving of these seemingly opposite dynamics. Accommodative people skills, assertive task skills—the science tells us effective leadership requires both.

Close the Gap

Now we know the kind of leadership skills we are supposed to develop. But how do we go about that development? The research reveals two practices that correlate to higher levels of leadership skills:

- Consistent reflection
- Intentional feedback

The Practice of Consistent Reflection

Shortly before our Minnesota lab manager Brian's world was disrupted at work, he had bumped into Dr. Michael Gervais, host of the *Finding Mastery* podcast.[13] Brian credits Gervais as the one who helped him get curious about mindfulness practice as a form of brain training. Gervais explained it's not the religious cult thing that skeptics are concerned about. Rather, the science of neuroplasticity and high-performance psychology asserts that we can reprogram our brains to new ways of thinking. We are not hardwired to be the same people we were at birth. You can change; you can develop.

So Brian tried it out. Through a certain amount of practice, he says, "I became aware of the imposter in my head: 'When is my boss going to fire me? Why would these people even listen to anything I have to say?' On and on and on. I knew it was there, but I chose to listen to it anyway."

He kept with it and eventually had an aha moment: "There was an inflection point where I pulled out of the pit of despair. I was able to say to myself, 'Wait a second. Okay, this self-doubt is really stupid. I see where we need to go. I see a path to get there. And you know what? I'm not going to get it perfect, but I got this.' That moment of self-care prompted even more energy. Color came back into my life."

If strong leadership is about applying the right balance at the right time, then it requires the perspective to do just that. The perspective to zoom out from your current situation, see yourself in a larger context, and then zoom back in to deploy the skill that best fits that context. This is the essence of building a reflective capacity, a core skill that correlates to measurably higher leadership effectiveness.

Joiner describes this capacity as a cycle of four actions:

1. **Assess situation and results.** Scan your environment and determine what issues (problems or opportunities) need your attention.
2. **Diagnose.** Once you have an issue in mind, think through the underlying cause or barrier.
3. **Set intentions.** Ask yourself, "What do you want?" and think through a pathway to get there.
4. **Take action.** Act with intent toward your goal.

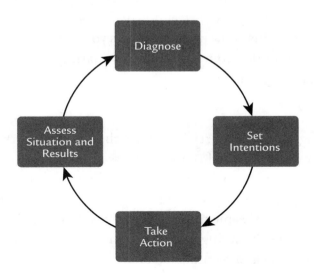

Move back to step 1, examine the results of your actions, and continue the cycle.

Joiner makes the point that everyone moves through this cycle regularly, but we do so unconsciously. Most of our daily decisions and actions are based out of instinct, habit, or autopilot.

This was the secret to Brian's breakthrough. He was iteratively listening to the narrative in his head, trying an action, and then testing that narrative against reality. Listen, try, test. Over and over until he could see the bigger picture.

Options for Practice

By now you might be thinking, "That sounds great, but *how* do I do it?" While meditation works for some, many of us just don't resonate with it. So let's turn to some successful CEOs for other ideas:

Just Pause

In one of the *Finding Mastery* episodes, Microsoft CEO Satya Nadella explains his own version of meditation each morning.[14] He wakes, sits up, puts his feet down, and pauses for ninety seconds. "It grounds you," he says. "It gets you in touch with yourself and the world around you. It's fascinating." No chants, no incense, no yoga. Just pause.

Exercise

Engaging in physical activity allows the brain to relax. Virgin Group founder Richard Branson starts every day with exercise. He prefers tennis, cycling, or kite surfing, because, he says, "Exercise puts me in a great mind frame to get down to business, and also helps me to get the rest I need each night. There's nothing more satisfying than knowing I have applied myself both physically and mentally every day."[15]

Soak

Buffer CEO Joel Gascoigne adds a little bonus to his morning exercise. "Most days I do 30 minutes of cardio (swimming or running) and then 10 minutes in the hot tub. Then I have a simple breakfast, before starting work. This gives me the best start I've found for my day, gets the endorphins going, and makes me feel refreshed and ready to make progress."[16]

Wake Up Early

By now you're wondering, where do these people find the time? Well, they get it in the mornings. Twitter's Jack Dorsey wakes up at 5 a.m. For Apple's Tim Cook, it's 3:45 a.m. Successful people don't sleep in.[17]

Journaling

Another option is to be your own coach, using your own language. The kinesthetic act of reading and writing can engage our fuller minds. The leadership mega-blogger Michael Hyatt has described journaling as a practice he has seen with almost all the high-powered leaders he's met. Curiously, his blog has served as a very public journal of his thoughts, making him a powerful example of how simple it can be to use the written word as a reflective tool.[18]

Retreats and Sabbaticals

The best way to sift out truth from noise is to get as far from the noise as possible. During his Microsoft days, Bill Gates would famously take a week off in the woods twice a year. He would spend almost all that time going through books and papers. "I would literally take boxes out to a beach place and sit there for a week reading them day and night and scribbling on them to put it entirely online."[19] Both academics and clergy have an established tradition to leave their day jobs for months on end, with the intent of rethinking the biggest questions of the universe. For you, it might be enough to take a weekend to yourself and see what percolates to the top of your mind, without the daily grind.

Executive Coaching

Bill Campbell was the "trillion dollar coach," according to the book of the same name.[20] This name was given to him by his clients—Steve Jobs, Eric Schmidt, Warren Buffett, among others. They all asserted that Campbell was a key reason for their successes at generating a collective trillion dollars of economic impact. Why did they speak so highly of him? One key theme was the tough questions he would ask CEOs, forcing them to check their assumptions and think more deeply about situations and choices. If it worked for them, coaching can help you too.

Here are some examples of how Emmit is working on building his reflective habits after receiving executive coaching.

Emmit
Executive

- "During my morning run last week, it occurred to me which vendor partnerships are worth bringing along on this transformation, and which I could live without."
- "Last month's journal entry shows me more bothered by the Q1 metrics than I am now. I wonder why my feelings have changed."
- "In our last coaching session, we talked about my desire to get more connected to my staff, and I still believe that's important. But with my schedule so much in demand, I guess I'm struggling with whom to disappoint in order to make that happen."
- "I took the weekend to go hiking without my family. It helped remind me what legacy I want in my career. I feel

more grounded against the inevitable bickering that awaits me at the office."

You have several options for activating your mind. Pick the ones that work for you, and start building the critical skill of reflective capacity.

The Practice of Intentional Feedback

Let's go back to Brian at the R&D lab. He was making progress on becoming the agile leader he wanted to become. But to go farther, he knew he needed an outside perspective. In 2018, the Global Scrum Gathering came to his home town of Minneapolis-St. Paul, bringing thousands of other agile champions with it. He decided to go check it out, see what others might have to say.

It was there he bumped into Michaele Gardner, an agile coach and adjunct instructor at the University of St. Thomas. They started a conversation about their respective experiences, what it means to them, and what it means to those they serve. Their contrasting perspectives were refreshing: he was the data, numbers, and math guy; she was the technologist with roots in psychology and counseling. That collaboration continued weeks after the conference through a series of conference calls, coaching each other in various challenges.

Then another inflection point happened. Brian describes it this way:

One day, I was sitting in my basement and we were on a teleconference, staring at a page on a shared screen. We were talking through the twelve principles of the Agile Manifesto and how they relate to leaders in an agile context. At one point during that conversation, I said, "What if we changed them? What if we rewrote the first principle so it said, 'Our highest priority is to be our best self so that we can help others be their best'?"

So, they did. Together they rewrote every single one of them, and something clicked. It was a rewarding experience to have their thinking challenged and reframed by a like-minded professional. But it didn't end there. Michaele was at another conference when she briefly met Kent Beck, a coauthor of those original agile principles. Kent helped push the conversation to the extreme— he brought it beyond "self care" and to "best self" outcomes. More feedback.

They posted their new principles online at agilebestself.com, which invited comments and encouragement from their colleagues. Still more feedback. They went a step further and delivered these principles to seventy of their peers at a local Twin Cities agile meet-up. Brian was dumbfounded at the positive response: "They showed up in the evening to come to this. That number of people was shocking to me. On a Tuesday night ? Who would do this? And so we delivered the workshop and when we got done, they all stood up and cheered."

All that happened because Brian took the intentional effort of going to that conference seeking professional feedback. He was discontent with his assumptions and perspectives, and needed an outside party to inject new information into his understanding of the world.

It turns out that deliberate practice of intentional feedback is a secret superpower for agile leaders. Let's go see what that is.

The Missing Feedback Loop

One of the fundamental ingredients of all agility is feedback. Virtually every one of the formal methods is designed to test some kind of hypothesis, evaluate the results of that test, and use the learning to inform the next steps.

- **The Lean Startup loop.** Ideas we build → code we measure → from data we learn → which impacts the ideas, restarting the loop. We engage the customer and the market to test the hypothesis that people actually want our stuff.
- **The DevOps loop.** Plan → code → build → test → release → deploy → operate → monitor → which impacts the plan, restarting the loop. We design the system to test the hypothesis that things actually work.
- **The Scrum loop.** Plan sprint goal → work the goal → review the goal → review the team's effectiveness → which informs the next goal. We schedule conversations to test the hypothesis that we are aligned on where we are versus where we should be.

Do you see what's missing from these feedback loops?
You are. The agility leader.

Comparison of Agile Feedback Loops

Agility Method	Feedback Loop	Hypothesis Tested	Source of Feedback
Lean Startup	Build ideas → Measure code → Learn from data → Repeat	The product has value	Customers
DevOps	Plan → Code → Build → Test → Release → Deploy → Operate → Monitor →	The product works	Product
Scrum	Plan sprint goal → Work sprint goal → Review sprint goal → Review the team	We are aligned on direction and progress	Overall team

Certainly, many of the methods target skills growth for the on-the-ground product teams. Techniques like pairing people together and team retrospectives are sometimes used to offer feedback to individual contributors, to help them grow on a personal professional level.

But what about the founder? The product owner? The transformation leader? The Scrum Master? What about Ted, Maria, or Emmit?

In all the push for iterating and improving everything we do, we have no formal mechanism for iterating and improving the leadership skills of those driving agility. We talk endlessly about the need for "servant leaders" to develop a "growth mindset" that "empowers the team." But we forgot to apply the same formalized feedback mechanisms to achieve that leadership goal.

"Okay, Jesse. Fair enough. But how do we do that?" Glad you asked.

Agility is missing a feedback loop for you, the agility leader.

Spinning Around in 360

One option to generate personalized feedback on how you're doing is to use the established technique of a 360 leadership survey. Here's how it works.

The survey asks some questions about how you approach your leadership work. Then those same questions are posed to your supervisors, mentors, peers, colleagues, and subordinates. Usually, the responses are anonymized to encourage candor and then aggregated into a team average. This allows for a contrast between how you perceive your performance versus how others perceive you.

Maria's Leadership 360 Review

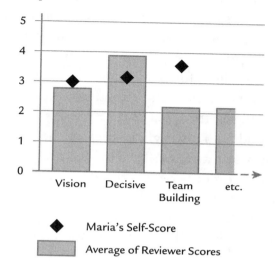

There are an uncountable number of 360 tools to choose from. You can choose from instruments created by the aforementioned Anderson and Adams or Joiner, or your company may have one that was developed in-house. Regardless of which you use, the intent is the same: to get feedback on how you are perceived as a leader. The chart shows what a snapshot of the results for Maria might look like.

A quick glance at the chart reveals a few conspicuous trends:

- **Self-awareness.** In the area of "vision," Maria's self-score is very close to those of the reviewers. Seeing yourself the way your colleagues do can be an asset in challenging situations, so that you don't overplay or underplay your role. Here, she agrees with her peers that she is only average at crafting and communicating vision, which can serve as an area of shared understanding.
- **Hidden strengths.** In the area of decisiveness, Maria scores herself lower than her reviewers do. This could

mean her team is grateful for her decisions, or it could mean she has a simmering lack of confidence in the decisions she does make. The tool doesn't tell us why there is a gap, only that a conversation could open up more possibilities for her.

- **Blind spots.** Maria's self-perception on team building is much higher than that of the reviewers in the area of team building. This might be because the team has recently grown and she's been too busy to create some collaborative glue between the older and newer team members. Or it could be she doesn't know where to begin with that mushy stuff. The data doesn't tell us the cause; it only tells us a conversation should happen here.

Maria
Manager

In addition to the quantitative scores, all good feedback instruments include qualitative comments. It's in the comments where the numbers start to show their true meaning to Maria:

"Maria has been stretched by the team's recent growth. She should consider delegating more or asking for help."

"We do a lot of work, so I'm grateful for Maria's decisiveness. That said, I do wish she would explain the big picture more often, so we know how she comes to those decisions."

"Maria is pretty vocal about focusing her team on execution and staying out of our strategy debates. But given her team's been making improvements in the organization, I think she's missing a key influence opportunity. I would like to see her flex more visionary skills."

As you can see, this kind of instrument can be powerfully insightful. But sometimes it can go in a negative direction. People can be unusually harsh in anonymous surveys. Below are some tips for approaching technology-driven feedback with success.

- **Discuss context, not truth.** One concern around 360s is that they are deeply contextual. If an adrenaline junkie scores Maria as 3 out of 5 on "quick decision making," that doesn't mean she's average at it. It only means that's how that one person sees her. And that is the point. Leadership perceived is leadership achieved. How people experience you may not be the fullest truth of who you are. That said, the perception of your leadership is how people are experiencing you, and knowing that is the first step to improving your impact.

- **Seek development, not assessment.** Whenever we use data to measure ourselves, it can be tempting to place a value judgment on whatever the numbers end up being. However, looking for high scores, or at least scores higher than others, can be a recipe for dysfunction. Academics, researchers, consultants, and seasoned leaders disagree on much, but they all agree on one thing: the point of 360s is not where you are, but rather what your next step is.

- **Choose your raters wisely.** One thing the Internet has taught us is that people can be really mean, especially when technology keeps us incognito. Using a tool to collect anonymous feedback can yield some false negatives, both in the qualitative numbers and the qualitative comments. Avoid that mess by choosing only those people whose perspective you trust and respect. Then give them a heads-up as to why you're asking them and what your goals are.

- **Use a coach.** Sometimes the feedback we get can be confusing or even crushing. Use a professional coach who can walk you through the results. A neutral perspective will help you sift away the distracting parts and get to the true substance that matters to you.
- **Chart a path forward.** The whole point of feedback is to adjust your path. As you go through your results with your coach, design a roadmap for building on your key growth area. Then schedule recurring check-ins with your coach or a few trusted colleagues. That way you can get sustained accountability on progress toward your goals.

Just Ask

Ted
Team Lead

If using a formal feedback instrument sounds like more hassle than it's worth, don't worry. You don't have to. You can use the old-fashioned approach to get feedback: go talk to people. Whether it's your boss, your peers, or your teams, you could get some very powerful insights by asking pointed questions. For team lead Ted, it could look like this:

- "How am I doing with walking the agile talk?"
- "Is the reason behind these practices clear to you? To others?"
- "Do I give enough 'space' for people to contribute?"
- "Does the team feel like I stick up for them?"
- "What does support from me look like?"

I know. These are tough questions. Potentially dangerous questions. How do we keep the conversation from getting weird? How can we make sure we get good, actionable information? To try this more informal feedback approach, leadership author Peter Bregman offers some very helpful tips:[21]

- **Be clear that you want honest feedback.** Let people know they're doing you a favor by being truthful. "Don't be nice," you can tell them. "Be helpful."
- **Focus on the future.** Avoid the drama, frustration, and guilt of the past. Instead, ask them to offer recommendations for being more effective going forward.
- **Probe more deeply.** Don't let them off the hook. If you sense there's something under the surface of a particular comment, ask, "And what else?" or "Tell me more about that." If you're not getting anything of substance, try being more specific: "How could I get more active participation from you in big-room planning?"
- **Listen without judgment.** This is the hardest part. If they offer something critical, it may well be a test to see if you're serious about hearing the truth. Try your best to redirect your natural feelings of defensiveness, injustice, or frustration. Remember, you asked for this awkwardness because you have a much bigger goal in mind. Whatever input you receive, express your gratitude for their honesty.
- **Write down what they say.** I love this suggestion for two reasons. First, it shows you're paying attention and respecting the input you receive. Second, it serves as an emotion safety net, giving you something to focus on when you hear something annoying. Simply write it down, be polite, and trust the process.

Remember, learning is the secret sauce to higher performance. Feedback is the means to achieve deep learning. Pursue it ruthlessly, regardless of whether you use a fancy psychometric instrument like a 360 survey or you start engaging people in honest dialogue.

An Agile Leadership Development Plan

Reflection and feedback. These are two development actions that can and should be pursued to expand your capacity as a leader and an agile practitioner. But don't limit yourself to just one action at one point in time. Growth is continuous and layered, so you want your own actions to be continuous and layered. Much the way DevOps, Lean Startup, and Scrum give us overlapping feedback loops of varying cadences, a personal development plan should feature the same.

On the website for this book is a template for designing such a plan. It is a simple worksheet to help you think through both sides of the equation.[22] Here is an example of how team leader Ted could use the worksheet to sketch a path forward.

Ted
Team Lead

"My biggest hurdle right now is the team's struggle with new technical practices. I guess the best source of feedback is the team itself. I could leverage our regular retrospectives, while also trying the occasional informal coffee chat. Regarding reflection, I'm not able to take much out of my day for, so perhaps if I leverage those chunks of time I already use—aha! What if I turned off the podcasts during my commute and just let my brain wander? That might be interesting. Also, I'm pretty reliable with my Saturday morning run, which could be used as some reflection time."

When Ted has finished scribbling on the worksheet, it looks like the figure.

Agile Leadership Development Plan		
Name: Ted the Team Lead		
Goal: Understand my team's struggle		
GET FEEDBACK		
Approach	Source	Frequency
Anonymized input for me during retrospective	The team	Monthly
One-on-one coffee	Maria, my manager & select team members	Bi-weekly; pace them out evenly
GET REFLECTION		
Approach		Frequency
Listen to classical music; calm down my brain		Evening commute
Morning run		Saturday mornings

Summary

In this chapter, we have done the hard work of looking in the mirror. Sometimes changes are happening, but the pace and degree feel wrong. We've learned about:

- **The leadership gap.** The expectation of agile leadership is to guide an organization through more volatility, uncertainty, complexity, and ambiguity (VUCA) than we ourselves can tolerate.
- **Defining effective leadership.** Research over the last century has shown us that navigating that VUCA requires a leadership style that is flexible from situation to situation, and balanced across the task-side and the people-side of daily work.
- **Closing the gap.** Rather than try to grow every leadership skill, we make the most progress focusing on the

practices of continuous reflection and intentional feedback.

Your growth is critical to your team's growth. Too often the agile conversation is about making "them" more innovative, collaborative, and responsive. Too often we forget about our own personal agile journey. As a result, the surveys identify over and over a key roadblock is "inadequate leadership support."

Unless you embark on your own journey, you will only get so much out of the teams on their journey. The good news is we now have a way forward

CHAPTER 8

Own the Narrative

Stories constitute the single most powerful weapon in a leader's arsenal.

—*Dr. Howard Gardner, professor, Harvard University*

I t was my job to lie about Agile.

At least, that's how it felt.

The CIO at a large bank was the proud sponsor of new credit card technology that enjoyed a very successful regional pilot. Now his vision was to scale the success of that technology across the entire North American region, with the help of a big-brand brick-and-mortar retailer. The bank would upgrade the technology, and the retailer would deploy it to hundreds of locations across the United States. Both sides were salivating at an opportunity that was valued at $2 billion.

But it was a complex undertaking. Success required support-ing every variation of state tax laws, adding support for Spanish speakers, integrating with the loyalty program, scaling the back office card operations, and moving the technology to a place that could handle the increased load. The good news was that the organizational cultures of both sides were steeped in analytical prowess. They were committed to getting it right, because the stakes were just too high. But the market pressure was also high. The retailer made it clear we needed to be done in twelve months. The estimated time required? Twenty-four months.

How do you overcome high risk and high complexity, and do so on such an aggressive timeline? The CIO had a plan: "Step 1, let's hire hundreds of people right away. Step 2, let's make them use agile methods. To get it right, and to get it fast, I want 80 percent of the entire backlog identified in the next three months. Once that backlog is approved by the retailer, then we can get started."

So they hired me to coach up the agility needed to get it all done. When I showed up to the office and heard this story, it took me a moment to digest what I'd just heard. Namely, we were in-structed to:

- Plan everything before we do anything.
- Then do it in a fraction of the time required.
- But everything is planned perfectly, so there won't be any mistakes.
- It was my job to coach everyone to make this happen.

This was the exact opposite of the flexible, incremental, experi-mental approaches associated with the lean/digital/innovation mindset. Yet somehow, a small army of technology profession-als were supposed to figure this all out.

So they came. Scrum Masters, project managers, program managers, analysts, technical writers, and testers began arriving en masse to our glass-enclosed office building in downtown Wilmington, Delaware. All eager to accomplish big things. They all looked at me expectantly. What imaginary management magic would we use to do the impossible? How is this anything like the agility we've seen in the wild? How is this not a violation of everything we stand for as modern innovators?

It was my job to advocate for an ill-conceived, confused, and inevitably doomed version of agility. It was my job to tell a story that was both impossible and unbelievable. They hired me for this, and it was my job to own it.

The Problem with Perception

As the agile leader, you have a different perception of reality than those you lead. The fact that you are driving change means you are moving people into a new reality they cannot yet see. They do not see the positive momentum that has been made; they only see the pain and frustration injected into their lives. Even more annoying, they don't yet have the mindset to see mistakes, pain, and awkwardness as necessary steps for growth. So the greatest value you can add right now is to help them make sense of it all.

- **The Boost.** Yes, it was good to score quick wins and spark momentum.
- **The Barrier.** And yet, the misperceptions and criticisms are mounting.
- **The Rebound.** So now, own the narrative.

The Pattern of Untapped Support

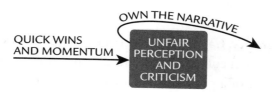

The Boost: Yes, It Was Good to Score Quick Wins and Spark Momentum

In the previous chapters, we've seen all the boosts available to get transformation started. You leveraged your role, installed best practices, ran several local pilots. You invested in a new culture. You captured several opportunities. You mobilized several teams. These were all quick wins to generate momentum that simply did not exist before.

The Barrier: And Yet, the Misperceptions and Criticisms Are Mounting

Despite all the progress made, people are fixated on those barriers we've discussed: People are frustrated that the progress isn't what they wanted it to be and are quick to criticize the changes made. Several of the vocal influencers aren't on board, the pilot teams' practices are poor, their results are limited. The culture isn't moving. There's too much going on, and they're challenging your leadership. Given everything that's been done, it's an ocean of negativity that simply doesn't make sense.

Perhaps your peers had a vision based on unrealistic outcomes. Perhaps they feel threatened by the changes to their role. Perhaps your pragmatism doesn't match the dogma they expected. Whatever the reason, you're facing a rising resistance.

The Rebound: So Now, Own the Narrative

The reason why the negativity is taking hold is because it contains a grain of truth. How do we take control of the story by acknowledging that truth and framing it as progress? We do that with an attitude and a technique:

- **Half empty, half full.** Sometimes complaints stem from logical consequences. Sometimes they are simply the result of a pessimistic attitude. We learn that both war veterans and improv theater performers know the difference between pessimism and pragmatism. That difference sets the stage for our talking points about change.

- **Framing the change narrative.** We borrow a storytelling template from fiction writing and import it into the leadership context.
- **Responding to common criticisms.** With these two concepts in hand, we will then be able to systematically deconstruct those recurring complaints.

We hear that storytelling is a key leadership skill, but nobody explains how to do it well. In this chapter, you will learn several tips and techniques for doing exactly that, and thereby enable the next level of transformation.

Half Empty, Half Full

The cliché is a cliché for a reason. It is an obvious recurring fact that different people view the same situation as good or bad. It's optimism or pessimism.

On the one hand, your agile journey has been mired with grumbling, compromise, and mistakes.

On the other hand, you have much to brag about. People are exposed to new ideas, which were previously totally foreign concepts. Teams are talking more to each other than they were before. We've forced dialogue about our traditions, and why we should change some of them. The deeper reality is that both perspectives are simultaneously real reflections of reality. Both are true.

The Stockdale Paradox

In his classic business book *Good to Great*, Jim Collins introduces what he calls the Stockdale Paradox, named after U.S. military

Leadership as Half-Empty versus Half-Full

veteran and former vice presidential candidate James Stockdale.[1] He was held as a prisoner of war in Vietnam for several years, starved and tortured with no reason to believe he'd make it out alive. Yet he survived. His strategy? He was able to overcome his adversity by building an attitude of simultaneous optimism and pragmatism.

In the book, Stockdale explained the mindset this way: "You must never confuse faith that you will prevail in the end—which you can never afford to lose—with the discipline to confront the most brutal facts of your current reality, whatever they might be."

Stockdale was able to avoid the temptation to give up and do so despite acknowledging the truth of his situation. He goes on to explain the dangers of not doing so:

> "Who didn't make it out? Oh, that's easy," he said. "The optimists. They were the ones who said, 'We're going to be out by Christmas.' And Christmas would come, and Christmas would go. Then they'd say, 'We're going to be out by Easter.' And Easter would come, and Easter would go. And then Thanksgiving, and then it would be Christmas again. And they died of a broken heart."

We need that Stockdale mindset, where we can acknowledge our struggles and keep hope for future possibilities. Before we learn how that gritty mindset applies to the business of change, let's take a quick detour to improv theater.

Yes, And

I've been through some improv theater and can personally vouch for what most people already know: it is a lot of fun. It's fun not just for the audience but for the performers as well. Coming up with creative responses to awkward situations creates great positive energy and, of course, often leads to some good laughs.

Curiously, it's not based solely on the individual talent of the participants; it's based on the philosophy called "Yes, And."[2] Even more curious, the secret of improv theater relates directly to Stockdale's philosophy on surviving a prison camp.

- **We verbalize "Yes!"** Improv performers acknowledge and embrace what your stage partner just said or did, no matter what. If they said a swear word, invented a new character, went off the storyline, danced a little jig, or anything else, we accept it as-is. No objecting to the unexpected turn of events. No complaining. No critiquing. It just is. This relates to the pragmatist part of the Stockdale mindset.
- **We verbalize "And!"** Next is offering something to the situation that moves the scene forward. Rather than halting movement with an objection or critique, we inject something additive. This relates to the optimist Stockdale, who did not accept his tragic conditions.

In the previous chapters, we've covered the *Untapped Agility* pattern for six common issues. However, our critics don't see the virtues of the progress made; they only see the pain points. So we need to inject a generative, additive, corrective attitude into the story. Specifically, we can use the phrase "Yes, And" not just as a conceptual guide but also as a template to articulate the Stockdale Paradox for each of those challenges:

- **For criticism over buy-in.** "Yes, I recognize that not everyone is on board with the change. And on the other hand, we've set a foundation of what agility is about. Therefore, I believe we can now align on what parts relate to us and why."
- **For criticism over impact.** "Yes, I recognize that agility so far is localized. And on the other hand, we've set a foundation for others to follow. Therefore, I believe we can now give it away to other champions."
- **For criticism over practices.** "Yes, I recognize that our practices are immature. And on the other hand, we've set a foundation to evolve from. Therefore, I believe we are now able to set the textbook aside and evolve into our own agility."
- **For criticism over workload.** "Yes, I recognize that we are always behind. And on the other hand, we've set a foundation of informed set of options to choose from. Therefore, I believe we are able to choose what to focus on right now and defer the rest."
- **For criticism over philosophy.** "Yes, I recognize that we're getting snapback to our old habits. And on the other hand, we've set a foundation of cultural/structure changes. Therefore, I believe now is the right time to add more substance to the change by blending in some structural/cultural elements."
- **For criticism over leadership.** "Yes, I recognize that I asked a lot from all of you. And on the other hand, we've set a foundation of growth we can be proud of.

Therefore, I believe now is the right time to reflect on our own personal leadership journeys."

As the champion of agility, your job is to tell a change story that inspires and motivates, but that is also is credibly grounded in reality. This is not easy, but it is doable. And if the "Yes, And" template doesn't sufficiently address a given critique, there is another reliable technique to try.

Framing the Change Narrative

In fiction storytelling, there are several ways to set up a story. One of the most recognizable is called the frame narrative, and the best way to explain it is with an example.

As the movie *Forrest Gump* opens, we see Forrest sitting on the iconic bus stop bench.[3] When a stranger sits next to him, Forrest proceeds to shares a solid hour's worth of flashbacks on his life, including his football years, his fighting in Vietnam, his running across the country, and his complex relationship with heartthrob Jenny. Eventually, the story catches up to the present day, where he's sitting on the bench, eagerly anticipating the reunion with Jenny. The flashbacks have created the tension, the excitement we feel for the rest of the story. The present, then the past, then back to the present with more context. The present *frames* the past.

From Fictional Stories toward Change Stories

When it comes to telling the change story, we do the same thing, with a twist. In fiction, context is created by the past. In change, context is created by the future. The present, then the future, then back to the present with more context.

1. **Clarify their perception.** Sometimes people voice their concerns inelegantly, especially when they're frustrated

or fearful. A simple follow-up question will allow you to get more data about the problem and avoid reacting to the poor packaging of the problem.

2. **Acknowledge the present.** This is empathy for the pessimist. Whatever the anxiety or objection, there's almost always a grain of truth. Calling it out and giving it air gives you credibility.

3. **Envision the future.** This is the time for the optimist. You have to believe there is light at the end of the tunnel. If you don't believe it, why should they? This is where you shine the light.

4. **Connect the future and present.** As before with Forrest Gump, now we can go back to our change story with a deeper context. Close out the narrative by returning to the task at hand.

Let's see how this framework of framing works in action.

Framing the Bank's Broken Agility

I knew it was going to be a tough meeting.

We were already a few weeks into the onboarding of the several hundred people needed to deliver this complex banking technology project in half the time needed. Every day they were seeing things that violated their agile sensibilities.

It was time to gather all the change agents into a private meeting. I had spent some time reflecting and preparing talking points. Now I had to communicate a narrative that would keep people moving forward but also keep them from losing their minds.

Clarify Their Perception

I opened the meeting. "Okay, gang. We're here to roll up our sleeves on the use of modern delivery methods to achieve the challenge put before us. Remember, we have a lot of work to do, so we may have to choose our battles. That said, what are you seeing there that worries or frustrates you?"

And boy, did they let me have it.

> "How can you justify a three-month planning phase? That's literally the opposite of iterative prototyping and incremental delivery. We're not allowed to begin delivering any work until the retailer agrees on literally everything to be delivered?"
>
> "I was hired to facilitate and empower a Scrum team, but I have not yet been assigned a team. Why am I here?"
>
> "Heck, the team I was assigned doesn't even honor my role. Their manager is overruling and contradicting me in every meeting. Doesn't he know I'm here to help him?"
>
> "Why are we estimating this backlog? Why measure the work in man-weeks when everyone knows that time-based estimation is unreliable?"
>
> "Jesse, it's so bad, the bank's agile transformation office said we will not be listed as an official agile project, because 'endorsing your approach will set the wrong tone for agility in this organization.'"

Acknowledge the Present

I responded with empathy, as well as offering some additional causes for their frustration they may not have realized.

> Yes, the majority of people on this program do not understand or appreciate your role. That's because, unlike you, they have no expertise or experience using modern methods. It will take time for us to teach them.

Yes, many of you do not yet even have a team. That's because we are still staffing up our teams. Until you have a quorum of people on a team, we can certainly use your help getting other existing teams moving on the backlog.

Yes, we've been asked to document a backlog of work we know very well will change as we move forward. That's because we have two organizations, both with perfectionist cultures. We have a long way to go to guide them to a better balance of planning and doing.

Yes, we're using traditional estimation techniques. That's because we simply don't have time to teach those strange and different agile estimation practices.

Envision the Future

Despite all that yuckiness, there were some very real bright spots I could see. So I shared them.

The good news is we have a lot to work with:

- The bank and the retailer are highly committed to working together. That "customer collaboration" value is very much in play.
- There is a lot of demand in customer-driven product development using techniques like customer journey maps, story maps, and a backlog taxonomy.
- The management team have designed pods, real teams that each involve all the critical departments.
- Those cross-functional pods are also generating their own estimates.

In some respects, we've already had an impact building an agile mindset. If we build on that, we can get to the other aspects that are missing. Specifically, leadership believes passing the next funding milestone will give us the green light to begin more iterative and incremental delivery.

Connect the Future and the Present

Then I brought them back to reality:

> The key is to build a just barely sufficient backlog to pass the next funding milestone. If it's okay, I'd like to focus the rest of our workshop on that topic.

Not a Silver Bullet

That message served as just enough air cover for us to move forward. We held several virtual training sessions, we leveraged the collaborative spirit on the program to generate a backlog, and we hit the short-term deadline for a funding review.

To be clear, there were still plenty of bumps and bruises along the way. A few staffers did leave the program, and the program's future was still very much up in the air. But it was a start. It was a vision. It was me taking ownership of the job I was given. To craft a message was just barely sufficient to keep the vast majority of people focused less on the frustrations of "bad agile" and focused more on the goals at hand.

This was just my story. For the rest of this chapter, we cover several other common criticisms you may come across. I'll show you how to frame a change story that contains some grounding pessimism and some inspiring optimism.

Common Criticisms

Now that we've seen the reframing technique in practice, let's examine how our personas could reframe the change narrative in the face of withering criticism.

"I'm taking the risk of going agile first, to lower the risk for others who might later."

Emmit
Executive

Emmit Responds to Criticism over Impact

Earlier in this book, we talked about the need to let go of control of your transformation in order to achieve greater impact. When you're ready to take that step, we will praise and encourage you as you aspire to move to the next stage. However, until you get there, you might get some flak for going forward alone.

Emmit has been piloting fancy techniques. However, his boss, the COO, has some concerns that it's a waste of time and a distraction. She says, "I've seen this movie before, and it doesn't go well. I don't want your team losing focus on core services."

Clarify Their Perception

Emmit starts with, "That sounds reasonable. Are you concerned that we're *doing* a lot of things, but our mindsets have not yet changed to a new way of *being?*"

The COO replies with new input: "No, it's understandable that mindset change takes time. Rather, I'm skeptical there's any value to your team using these techniques in a silo, unless you have the whole organization doing them as well, and we're just not ready for that scale of change."

Acknowledge the Present

Emmit replies, "That is a fair point. It would be ideal if our whole group was able to collaborate together. We'd be able to speed up work moving across all the departments. My team's improvements will not have that kind of impact. Moreover, I agree with your point about readiness. Jason, Marcos, and Cindy all have their teams doing a lot right now, and an organization-wide improvement effort would be a distraction."

Envision the Future

Then Emmit appeals to what motivates the COO: results and risk aversion. "However, there is a method to the madness. First, I believe our talent can find some real opportunities on the ground, just in customer service alone. I don't want to jinx it, but initial indications are rather promising. Second, these new ways of working should only be shared with the other leaders if we've first proved they can add tactical value. Given the other leaders don't have my familiarity with agile methods, I don't think they should take the risk of change until I've first validated my hypothesis."

Connect the Future and the Present

Emmit continues, "I've put guardrails in place that ensure they can experiment a little and still hit their targets. We're moving forward cautiously. You know me well enough to know I take my targets seriously. If you give me a little leeway here, we'll have more information soon enough to see where it goes."

Ted Responds to Criticism over Practices

In chapter 4, we discovered two key principles to help us position our poor practices within a bigger picture:

- Find your legs as you crawl, walk, run into the practices.
- Find your own agile practices that fit your context.

Ted
Team Lead

"We are evolving our practices.
Crawl, walk, run."

These principles will help you own the fact that you're using these methods in an unconventional way. Here's an example of how crafting a crawl, walk, run story can change the perception of those poor practices.

Team lead Ted has a new addition to the team, Geri the Genius, who says, "I'm new to this team, so I've waited a week to highlight this problem. But based on my experience, I can tell you that's not a proper Kanban practice. You're missing half the data."

Clarify Their Perception

Ted starts with, "That sounds interesting. Are you concerned that we're not tracking blockers?"

Geri replies with new input: "No. That's not a problem; we can just talk through those in our daily stand-up. Rather, I'm frustrated that you're only posting maintenance requests. Unless you put all the work up there, we can't see the flow, and that's the whole point of the technique."

Acknowledge the Present

Now Ted sees where to take the conversation. "That is a fair point. It would be better for our own internal work assignments if we posted all our work in the same place. However, you may not know that our boss is very anxious about doing that. This board is very visible, and if we put our whole mess up there, he'll get heat he's not ready to handle."

Envision the Future

Ted continues, "Instead, we're moving forward cautiously. First we'll get good at visualizing, expediting, and measuring those maintenance requests. Meanwhile, we'll get better at slicing our projects into smaller work items, and gradually add a few of those smaller items on the board. Eventually, we'll have both habits and data that are credible enough to include all our work in the technique."

Connect the Future and the Present

Ted concludes his pitch: "So, we've agreed as a team to suffer the short-term annoyance of slower projects and broken Kanban, and work our way to a better place. I take comfort in knowing the deeper principle of the Kanban method is to start where you are and get better one small step at a time. Is that something you can support?"

Maria Responds to Criticism over Leadership

In chapter 7, we saw Brian's journey to overcome imposter syndrome. On the other hand, some of us are brimming full of confidence, barreling forward with our own ideas and emotions, and create unintended impact on the teams we influence. In either extreme, your agile-minded boss may not appreciate the time it's taking you to grow into the right mindset.

Maria
Manager

"I agree I have growing to do. I'm hoping my progress can inspire my team."

Let's say Maria is tasked with driving the agile transformation, and the conversation gets awkward when her boss, the vice president, says, "I've called you in here because I'm concerned about how you're doing in your role. You're making great progress installing some of the processes. But you're too assertive with this change effort."

Clarify Their Perception

Maria knows this is going to be tough. "Okay, I'm listening. Can you give me an example?"

The VP dives right in and shares a recent complaint: "Well, one project manager came to me last week rather shaken. He shared how the two of you got into an argument during a kaizen meeting. He was asking me whether I'd heard about the episode and whether he'd done anything wrong."

Acknowledge the Present

Maria knows it's time for some candor. "Yes, that happened, and I know who you're talking about. He made a point that his suggestions haven't been implemented by the change committee, and I just . . . I just reacted. I didn't realize it at first, but eventually I felt bad about shutting down the conversation. I apologized to him privately on Monday, and we came up with some ideas for moving forward. I'm sorry the timing of the events got you involved. The truth is, I'm aware I have some liabilities that are impacting my effectiveness."

Envision the Future

Maria continues, "For the last couple months, I've engaged an executive coach, at my own expense. My coach is helping me surface a handful of insecurities I didn't even realize I had. They started after I took this role. Between the change resistance, the dilution of the practices, and the demands for support, I've had to juggle more frustration than ever before. The good news is I'm starting to catch my anxieties before they show up as reactions. Last week was one that got away from me. I'm trying to be honest about the journey. The hope is by doing so, I can rebuild some relational capital. Heck, it might even serve as an example to others of the personal growth this transformation can require."

Connect the Future and the Present

The VP's body language shows him to be intrigued, so Maria continues. "Listen, I appreciate the accountability. I need as much feedback as I can get on this. I know I can only serve in this role if I do it well, and I don't want to be a liability. If you're willing to let me, I'd like to keep going into the challenge."

Summary

In this chapter, we've tackled what to do when your boosts all incur recurring criticism and unfair perceptions. To craft a better story, we've learned about:

- **Half empty, half full.** The mindsets of a prisoner of war and an improv performer are strangely, similarly effective. Yes, acknowledge the unexpected, unwanted reality. And add a creative, positive step forward.
- **Framing the change narrative.** The same storytelling technique used in the movie *Forrest Gump* can be adjusted to tell the fuller story of your transformation.
- **Responding to common criticisms.** It turns out the specific criticisms are not the challenging part. All of them can fit the talking point techniques we've explored. The hard part is knowing the deeper truths you are marching toward. If you know that, you can take the heat with more confidence.

CHAPTER 9

Transforming Your Transformation

In the previous chapters, we have discussed a recurring pattern around leading change. Whether it is buy-in, impact, practices, workload, philosophy, your actual leadership skills, or even just the perception of those skills, we have seen this pattern:

- **The Boost.** Yes, leaders start with the right things.
- **The Barrier.** And yet, we experience common, frustrating barriers.
- **The Rebound.** But a leadership move in the seemingly opposite direction will yield further gains.

To paint the picture another way, the next figure shows all the untapped agility patterns.

If it feels like a lot, it is. Organizations are complex organisms. Even if it's not a surprise that there are so many things to keep in mind, it's still a bit overwhelming.

Therefore, in this final chapter, we will cover the topics you need to gain confidence and clarity in moving forward. Specifically, we will look at:

- **Untapped principles.** These are the recurring themes that have emerged over the seven leadership patterns.
- **Curveballs and landmines.** Here we share several additional frustrations and barriers that can further complicate the ones already discussed.

The Seven Untapped Agility Patterns

The BOOST	The BARRIER	The REBOUND
Leverage your role	They're not on board	Stop selling, start aligning
Take initiative	Siloed impact	Give it away
Install best practices	They're doing it wrong	Throw the textbook away
Seize opportunities	Overcommitted	Master "no"
Consistent philosophy	Reverting to old habits	Attack culture and structure together
Mobilizing them	The change feels wrong	Look in the mirror
Quick wins and momentum	Unfair perception and criticism	Own the narrative

- **Getting going.** Finally, we list some concrete suggestions for taking action.

Let's see how we go about transforming our transformations.

Untapped Principles

If you felt that there were some similarities among the seven transformation patterns we've discussed, I agree with you. Beyond the core untapped agility pattern itself, a few pervasive themes have emerged.

Embrace the Roller Coaster

Change is a messy business. One overarching theme we've seen across these seven patterns is the high of getting started, followed by the low of frustration, followed by the high of new opportunity. Transformation does not go in a straight line, it goes up and down.

Unfortunately, most of us have been trained as leaders to develop the single right plan at the very beginning. Failure, therefore, is either the result of inadequate planning, incompetent execution, or both. Well, that might be true for certain business functions like onboarding a new hire or securing a line of credit, but it's simply the wrong analytical mindset for organizational change.

Recall in chapter 7 that Brian made the right move by installing practices he learned during a training workshop. However, when successes started compounding, it quickly felt out of control. Eventually, he grew new personal leadership capacities that allowed him to get on top of the chaos. Elsewhere, we learned with the J-curve that many human systems go up and then down and then up again. The principle here is to embrace the mess, to get comfortable being uncomfortable. Leadership itself is hard enough, but when you start venturing into new realities, the path of leadership starts to look more like a roller coaster.

It's Never Done Right the First Time—Just Start

Change is easy in the beginning. We haven't tried anything yet, which means we haven't screwed anything up yet. Then, as the roller coaster starts, we start feeling a few bruises and shocks. Some of us will quickly brush off that initial surprise and continue plowing forward a little bit longer. But in the end, all of us will run into frustrations when it comes to leading the kind of transformative changes we want to last. In chapter 4, we heard the story of navy commander Dave Marquet, who found the one unique way his specific leadership team wanted to be empowered. However, another fascinating part of his story is that it was his third time attempting to build such a transformative culture. He tried making similar cultural changes in his previous assignments, with very frustrating results. In chapter 5, we saw Luis encouraging all-hands retrospective, which revealed negative feedback on some of the initial changes made.

Bottom line? Your first attempts will never be perfect, but they will be close enough to get started. Let go of your need to figure it out before getting started.

It's Never Too Late to Pivot

Just because you have a plan doesn't mean you have to follow it. General Dwight D. Eisenhower famously said, "In preparing for battle, I have always found that plans are useless but planning is indispensable." Perhaps you are already well into a comprehensive transformation roadmap; you've successfully formalized a center of excellence and rolled out a very robust practices playbook. After reading this book, you are probably rethinking that current state and wondering if you just made a whole bucket load of mistakes.

Don't forget, those are not mistakes. They are the first steps. But now is very much the right time to begin thinking about your next adjustment, your next pivot on the transformation journey. If you're worried about how it might look for you to alter your strategy, don't. In chapter 8, we offered guidance on how to craft a story that includes the past, the present, and the future. The best way to emulate the adaptability that you are trying to encourage in your organization is to adapt the change itself as you gather new information, gain allies, and score wins.

"Done" Is in the Eye of the Beholder

I recently volunteered at a conference booth offering free advice to change practitioners. One agile coach, John (not his real name), came to the booth seeking tips for a key frustration: he was bored. He had built a really strong transformation team, which had achieved some exciting new capabilities over the last couple of years. However, now that the more difficult problems had been solved, his team was able to take more and more responsibility, leaving him underutilized. He was fully convinced he was doing something wrong. I asked him, "What if all this means that you've done what you came to do?" His eyes lit up with the possibility, and we started brainstorming new ideas and new places for his career to go.

Then there's General Electric. We've mentioned them a couple of times in this book. The question of whether their $4 billion transformation was a success depends on whom you ask. On the one hand, the new digital capabilities across the corporate family of companies have yielded a modern wave of innovation that would not have otherwise happened. On the other hand, that innovation was not enough to overcome some of the more fundamental systemic issues that have since caused the stock price to suffer and some of those companies to be sold off. And yet, GE's transformation efforts continue. At the time of the writing of this book, I facilitated a leadership workshop at GE Aviation, where senior leaders were talking about how to continue evolving into a productized organization. For many, there's a lot more work to be done, despite all of the work done so far.

So here's the principle to keep in mind: if you think you're done, someone in your leadership team might disagree. Conversely, if you think you've only just begun, you might be shocked to hear your peers say further investment is no longer justified.

Curveballs and Landmines

The seven frustrations and barriers we've covered throughout this book are not the only ones you will come up against. There are a few others that can emerge on their own or further aggravate any of those already discussed. I could write another entire book on these, but I include some quick thoughts here, so that you don't feel completely alone or completely ambushed.

The New Boss Has Maria Feeling in Limbo

Maria
Manager

"New leadership has been installed, threatening to alter or even undo all our transformation efforts. What do I do?"

First, get on the new leader's radar. Schedule time to walk through new organizational results achieved with your agile/digital/DevOps/lean transformation. Let me emphasize here that you lead with the results, and talk about the technical details secondarily. As you talk, categorize the new leader into one of these three categories:

- **Mostly aligned.** The boss appreciates the new outcomes (speed, quality). She may have some opinions about adjusting the organizational structure, culture, or practices. But mostly you're on the same page.
- **Mixed minds.** In this case, the boss likes some parts of your story but is not on board with other parts.
- **Mostly against.** Here, the boss fundamentally disagrees. She may say, "I've been placed in this role exactly because the transformation isn't moving fast enough." Or she may say, "That's all well and good, but any solid organization needs to respect the chain of command, and that's what we're going to emphasize." You leave this conversation knowing you no longer have the support you used to have.

My experience tells me each of these is equally likely. Regardless of which category your boss fits into, you will need to choose your battles. Knowing the leader's position will help you choose the right battles going forward. Go back and study the ideas in chapter 2 to help with that.

For the leader who is mostly against your changes, you have two choices: wait it out or leave. Some organizations have a lot of churn at the management levels with frequent reorganization and reassignments. In these cases, it could be a wise move to hold firm, lay low, and then try again with the next leader. If you sense this new person is going to be around for a while, it might be time to find a new work environment that better aligns with your values and dreams.

The Mass Exodus Has Emmit Worried

Emmit
Executive

"I've lost my best talent over the last few months. This transformation was supposed to improve engagement and retention, and it's had the opposite effect. What's going on?"

Professionals have a fairly high pain tolerance for frustrating work environments. One survey shows that nearly half of all US employees are essentially ready to leave their company right now.[1] Common motivators range from lack of advancement opportunities to work flexibility and the relationship with a direct supervisor.

So more employees than you think are already on the brink of leaving. Then add to that mix the reality of unexplained changes in how business is done. When we talk about building a modern culture of self-organizing teams, supervisors are left wondering how they can contribute value. When we talk about expecting technology professionals to perform both development and testing responsibilities, they interpret that as an excuse to reduce head count.

When I attended my first workshop on agile methods in 2006, Scrum cofounder Ken Schwaber told us to expect a third of our staff to opt out of the change by leaving their jobs and half of management to leave as well. Those were his own anecdotal estimates, but the point holds: tension plus change is a recipe for attrition.

So what do we do?

1. **Prepare for the blowback.** Have the easiest answers ready. "No, this is not a reduction in workforce." "No, we are not changing all our practices at once." "No, we are not doing this everywhere right away; it will start with pilots here and here."
2. **Overcommunicate.** In chapter 2, we talked about the criticality of messaging and repetition.
3. **Accept that some will not journey with you.** No matter how hard you try, there will always be a meaningful minority of people who are just not able to go through the change. Let them leave. Their absence will create the space for new people who better align to the organization's future.

The Last Straw Has Ted Discouraged

Ted
Team Lead

"I've been at this for a while, but it's just not going well. Between the disappointment and the criticism, I'm ready to throw in the towel. How do you know when enough is enough?"

1. **Remember that pain is part of growth.** Let's go back to that J-curve, where we learned that things get worse before they get better. In case it's not obvious, this sucks. Recall in chapter 2, Gretchen waited years before things started to settle into a new groove.
2. **Find a support system.** Connect with others in the office who think like you do. Even if their tips and

suggestions don't land perfectly, the emotional support will keep you from losing your mind. If you are the only one at your office, then go to a local meetup to find your kindred spirits.

3. **Consider leading somewhere else.** Sometimes you try and try, but people don't come around. At some point, you collect enough data on where your team is at and whether you can wait long enough for them to change far enough fast enough for you to thrive. If your message simply isn't landing with others, it might be time to move to another place to bring your transformational energies. If that idea makes you cringe, consider whether finding a new role in a new department or new company is really any more painful than the daily pushback. Sometimes it's time to move on.

Layoffs Make Maria Wonder If It Was Her Fault

Maria
Manager

"Our company has been struggling for a while, so we started a digital transformation to reclaim our competitive edge. Unfortunately, after a year of training our people and running pilots, the senior leadership laid off 30 percent of the workforce. Was our transformation a failure?"

No, it wasn't your fault. Rather, it was too little too late. In chapter 8, we explored my experiences at a bank using modern methods incorrectly. Granted, I was able to reclaim some transformational momentum by reframing the narrative, and that kept the program going for a little while longer. Unfortunately, the product venture was too large and ambitious to pass an incremental funding review. As a result, the program was canceled, several team leads and managers were reassigned to other departments and programs, and my own consulting engagement was dissolved. However, despite the collapse of that program, I consider the frustrating turn of events to be a meaningful success.

- **First, organizational agility matters just as much as team agility.** The bank saved a ton of money by killing a runaway agile project. It turns out they had already implemented the progressive Lean Startup process of metered funding, which we discussed in chapter 5. All of my coaching efforts could not prevent senior leadership from barreling forward on a failed strategy. Instead, modern methods helped accelerate that failure so that we could all move on with the rest of our lives.

- **Second, all those people increased their agile IQ.** The employees that got reassigned are moving into their new roles with a deeper knowledge and experience of modern methods. They know how to write specifications from a customer perspective, they have felt first-hand the power of cross-functional teams, and many have had their first exposure to short iterative work cycles. That kind of experience will be the foundation for them to contribute more innovation, creativity, and agility in their professional futures.

For these reasons and a few others, I believe there's no such thing as a truly failed transformation. There are only transformations whose benefits are not the ones anticipated.

There's no such thing as a truly failed transformation. There are only transformations whose benefits are not the ones anticipated.

Getting Going

The knowledge gained in this book is an important first step. As the saying goes, "Knowledge is power." But I'd like to add that knowledge without action is a waste of time and money. The laws of physics favor objects in motion, so it's time for you to get moving.

Get Free Resources

This book comes with a toolkit of simple tools to get you started, free of charge. On the website UntappedAgility.Com, you will find, among other things:

- Blank copies of the agile leadership canvas to fill out at your next leadership team meeting
- Talking points for each of the three personas to begin directing the change narrative
- *Untapped Agility* book club materials to spark conversation with your colleagues
- *Untapped Agility* graphics you can use in presentation decks

Get Outside Help

If there's one thing that is universal, it's success as a team sport. You cannot do this alone. In order to import and adopt those organizational capabilities you envy in others, you need to go ask them how they did it. Here are some tips on how to do that.

Pursue Learning

You cannot do something until you understand it. You cannot understand something until you know about it. I am a part of the Agile Leadership Journey collective, a group of global thought leaders offering education and training programs to equip leaders in their efforts to achieve organizational agility. You can learn more at AgileLeadershipJourney.com.

Find a Coach

At VirtuallyAgile.com, we are a coalition of coaches and advisors who have made it our life's work to help you through this stuff. Reach out to us, and we will match you with a guide who has the expertise that fits your situation.

Build a Coalition

Another success pattern is to build a coalition of leaders in similar contexts pursuing a transformation goal similar to yours. Whether through your own initiative or with the help of your coach, reach out to your peers in your space and offer to exchange tips and ideas. Certainly you want to avoid divulging any competitive or proprietary secrets, but you will find there are plenty of people ready to support each other on this journey.

Untapped Agility

In this book, we have explored seven moves to help transformation leaders overcome the most common frustrating barriers to further organizational maturity. Whether you are most like Ted the Team Leader, Maria the Manager, or Emmit the Executive, these moves can offer you more confidence and credibility driving a better way of working.

Now you have what you need to get going. No more excuses. Go transform your transformation, and find that untapped agility.

Notes

Chapter 1

1. Scott Kirsner, "The Barriers Big Companies Face When They Try to Act Like Lean Startups," *Harvard Business Review*, August 16, 2016, https://hbr.org/2016/08/the-barriers-big-companies-face-when-they-try-to-act-like-lean-startups.

2. Eric Ries, *The Startup Way: How Modern Companies Use Entrepreneurial Management to Transform Culture and Drive Long-Term Growth* (New York: Currency, 2017).

3. Manifesto for Agile Software Development, http://agilemanifesto.org/.

4. Annual State of Agile Report, https://www.stateofagile.com/.

5. Agile Alliance, Experience Reports, https://www.agilealliance.org/resources/experience-reports/.

6. The origins of the DevOps movement are an inspiring read about grassroots disruption. The full story is available at https://theagileadmin.com/what-is-devops/.

7. Imarc Group, "DevOps Market: Global Industry Trends, Share, Size, Growth, Opportunity and Forecast 2019–2024," https://www.imarcgroup.com/devops-market.

8. 2014 State of DevOps Report, https://puppet.com/resources/whitepaper/2014-state-devops-report.

9. Prosci, Change Management and Agile Report, https://store.prosci.com/change-management-agile-report.html.

10. 2018 State of DevOps Report, https://puppet.com/resources/report/2018-state-devops-report/.

11. The Coding Gnome, "Agile Is Dead (Long Live Agility)," March 4, 2014, https://pragdave.me/blog/2014/03/04/time-to-kill-agile.html.

12. Steve Blank, "Is the Lean Startup Dead?" September 5, 2018, https://steveblank.com/2018/09/05/is-the-lean-startup-dead/.

13. See this great rebuttal from the innovation firm Strategyzer: Tendayi Viki, "Lean Startup Is Dead—Long Live Lean Startup," March 19, 2017, https://www.forbes.com/sites/tendayiviki/2017/03/19/lean-startup-is-dead-long-live-lean-startup/.

14. For the most vocal examples, see Ron Jeffries's blog series on "Dark Scrum," https://ronjeffries.com/categories/dark-scrum/; Martin Fowler's keynote about the agile industrial complex, https://martinfowler.com/articles/agile-aus-2018.html; and the FansOfLess.com community protest.

15. Steve Blank, "Why GE's Jeff Immelt Lost His Job—Disruption and Activist Investors," November 1, 2017, https://steveblank.com/2017/11/01/why-ges-jeff-immelt-lost-his-job-disruption-and-activist-investors/.

16. Forbes Insights and Scrum Alliance, "The Elusive Agile Enterprise: How the Right Leadership Mindset, Workforce and Culture Can Transform Your Organization," 2018, https://www.scrumalliance.org/ScrumRedesignDEVSite/media/Forbes-Media/ScrumAlliance_REPORT_FINAL-WEB.pdf.

17. For the detailed analysis, go to our free resources at the book website, UntappedAgility.com.

Chapter 2

1. Even if you've practiced Scrum in the past, I strongly recommend you read the official description. It contains aspirational values and practices that most don't know about. Check it out here: https://scrumguides.org/.

2. Personal interview, May 31, 2019.

3. Jeffrey M. Hiatt, *ADKAR: A Model for Change in Business, Government and Our Community* (Loveland, CO: Prosci, 2006).

4. Kotter, "8-Step Process for Leading Change," https://www.kotterinc.com/8-steps-process-for-leading-change/.

5. Chip Heath and Dan Heath, *Switch: How to Change Things When Change Is Hard* (New York: Broadway, 2010).

6. Simon Sinek, "How Great Leaders Inspire Action," TED talk, September 2009, https://www.ted.com/talks/simon_sinek_how_great_leaders_inspire_action.

7. Gerald Zaltman, "The Subconscious Mind of the Consumer (and How to Reach It)," https://hbswk.hbs.edu/item/the-subconscious-mind -of-the-consumer-and-how-to-reach-it.

8. Rick Rieder, "Tech Adoption Rates Have Reached Dizzying Heights," *Market Realist*, December 24, 2015, https://marketrealist.com/2015/12 /adoption-rates-dizzying-heights/.

9. CIPD, Megatrends, https://www.cipd.co.uk/knowledge/work/trends /megatrends.

10. Michael Sheetz, "Technology Killing Off Corporate America: Average Life Span of Companies Under 20 Years," CNBS, August 24, 2017, https://www.cnbc.com/2017/08/24/technology-killing-off -corporations-average-lifespan-of-company-under-20-years.html.

11. Scott D. Anthony, S. Patrick Viguerie, Evan I. Schwartz, and John Van Landeghem, Innosight, *2018 Corporate Longevity Forecast: Creative Destruction Is Accelerating*, https://www.innosight.com/insight/creative -destruction/.

12. Kim Gerard, "It's Not Nagging: Why Persistent, Redundant Com- munication Works," *Working Knowledge*, April 18, 2011, https://hbswk .hbs.edu/item/its-not-nagging-why-persistent-redundant -communication-works.

13. My favorite family of assessment tools is at https://Comparative Agility.com. It's a commercial product, but it's completely free to those who hold certain certifications from the Scrum Alliance.

Chapter 3

1. Robin Dymond, Twitter, March 12, 2018, https://twitter.com /robindymond/status/973292504815583233.

2. Eliyahu M. Goldratt, *The Goal: A Process of Ongoing Improvement* (Great Barrington, MA: North River, 1984).

3. Mike Cottmeyer, "The Secret to Organizational Agility," https:// www.leadingagile.com/2008/12/the-secret-to-organizational-agility/.

4. *Accelerate State of DevOps 2019*, https://services.google.com/fh/files /misc/state-of-devops-2019.pdf.

5. *Accelerate State of DevOps 2019*, https://services.google.com/fh/files /misc/state-of-devops-2019.pdf.

6. 13th Annual State of Agile Report, https://www.stateofagile.com /#ufh-c-473508-state-of-agile-report.

7. Project Management Institute, "PMI Talent Triangle," https://www.pmi.org/learning/training-development/talent-triangle.

8. Scott Berkun, *The Year Without Pants* (San Francisco: Jossey-Bass, 2013).

9. Laszlo Bock, *Work Rules!* (New York: Hachette, 2015).

10. Bernard Marr, "How Accenture and Deloitte Got Rid of Performance Reviews—and You Can Too," LinkedIn, August 16, 2015, https://www.linkedin.com/pulse/how-accenture-deloitte-got-rid-performance-reviews-you-bernard-marr/.

11. Scrum Alliance, "Scrum Alliance® Adds Chief ScrumMaster Melissa Boggs Alongside Chief Product Owner Howard Sublett," January 22, 2019, https://medium.com/scrum-alliance/scrum-alliance-announces-chief-scrummaster-cf4be412a0dc.

12. Scrum Alliance, *Unscripted*, https://www.scrumalliance.org/unscripted.

Chapter 4

1. The Scrum Master role is defined in the Scrum framework. See https://scrumguides.org/.

2. 13th Annual State of Agile Report, https://www.stateofagile.com/#ufh-c-473508-state-of-agile-report.

3. Ian Bremmer, *The J Curve: A New Way to Understand Why Nations Rise and Fall* (New York: Simon & Schuster, 2007).

4. John Banmen, "The Satir Model: Yesterday and Today," *Contemporary Family Therapy* 24, no. 1 (2002): 7–22, https://link.springer.com/article/10.1023/A:1014365304082.

5. According to the 13th Annual State of Agile Report, the word "Scrum" and its variants ("Scrum/XP Hybrid" and "Scrumban") are used by nearly three-fourths of all professionals in the agile movement.

6. "What Is ScrumBut?" https://www.scrum.org/resources/what-scrumbut.

7. The Clever PM, "Why 'ScrumBut' Shouldn't Be a Bad Word," June 8, 2017, http://www.cleverpm.com/2017/06/08/why-scrumbut-shouldnt-be-a-bad-word/.

8. Jurgen Appelo, "ScrumButs Are the Best Part of Scrum," September 2, 2009, https://noop.nl/2009/09/scrumbuts-are-the-best-part-of-scrum.html.

9. L. David Marquet, *Turn the Ship Around!* (New York: Penguin, 2012).

10. Project Management Institute, *A Guide to the Project Management Body of Knowledge*, 6th ed. (Newtown Square, PA: Project Management Institute, 2017).

Chapter 5

1. 13th Annual State of Agile Report, https://www.stateofagile.com /#ufh-c-473508-state-of-agile-report.

2. 2019 Accelerate State of DevOps Report, https://cloud.google.com /devops/state-of-devops/.

3. Jeff Sutherland and J. J. Sutherland, *Scrum: The Art of Doing Twice the Work in Half the Time* (New York: Crown, 2014).

4. Personal interview, June 3, 2019.

5. Jim Collins and Morten T. Hansen, *Great by Choice* (New York: HarperCollins, 2011).

6. Metered funding is explained in detail in Eric Ries, *The Startup Way* (New York: Currency, 2017).

7. The book *Work Rules!* details the many organizational experiments that Google has run. Laszlo Bock, *Work Rules!* (New York: Hachette, 2015).

8. Scaled Agile Framework, https://www.scaledagileframework.com/.

9. In a March 22, 2020, private interview with Scaled Agile Fellow: the planning iteration (25h) + four iteration plannings, standups, reviews, and retros (24h) + ongoing refinement (10h) = 59 out of 400 work hours = 15%. For a more detailed breakdown, go to the book website Untapped Agility.com.

10. Gartner Glossary, "Bimodal," https://www.gartner.com/en /information-technology/glossary/bimodal.

11. Clint Boulton, "Why Digital Disruption Leaves No Room for Bimodal IT," *CIO*, May 11, 2017, https://www.cio.com/article/3196037 /why-digital-disruption-leaves-little-no-room-for-bimodal-it.html.

12. *Agile Practice Guide* (Newtown Square, PA: Project Management Institute, 2017). Also available as a free download to Agile Alliance members (https://www.agilealliance.org/agile-practice-guide/) and PMI members (https://www.pmi.org/pmbok-guide-standards/practice -guides/agile).

13. William Ury, *The Power of a Positive No* (New York: Bantam, 2007).

Chapter 6

1. Manifesto for Agile Software Development, http://agilemanifesto. org.

2. Zappos aspires to be transparent about their Holacracy experiment on their website (https://www.zapposinsights.com/about/holacracy). But not everyone believes it was worth it: see Jennifer Reingold, "How a Radical Shift Left Zappos Reeling," *Fortune*, March 4, 2016, http:// fortune.com/zappos-tony-hsieh-holacracy/.

3. Craig described his reorg process in a 2015 speech in London, starting at 36:02, https://www.youtube.com/watch?v=phOCA3my Nws.

4. Jeff Sutherland, Scott Downey, and Björn Granvik, "Shock Therapy: A Bootstrap for Hyper-Productive Scrum," http://ieeexplore.ieee.org /document/5261105/.

5. Boris Groysberg and Michael Slind, "Leadership Is a Conversation," *Harvard Business Review* (March 2012), https://hbr.org/2012/06 /leadership-is-a-conversation.

6. Brené Brown, *Dare to Lead* (New York: Random House, 2018).

7. Charles Duhigg, *Power of Habit* (New York: Random House, 2012).

8. Tim Harford, *Adapt: Why Success Always Starts with Failure* (Boston: Little, Brown, 2011).

9. Federal News Network, "OPM Director John Berry Promises Big Changes for Hiring, Retention, Retirement," April 15, 2010, https:// federalnewsradio.com/all-news/2010/04/opm-director-john-berry -promises-big-changes-for-hiring-retention-retirement/.

10. Richard Cheng and Bridget Dongarra, "Super Product Ownership: Creating and Scaling Product Ownership in the Federal Government," https://agile2016.sched.com/event/6edL/super-product-ownership -creating-and-scaling-product-ownership-in-the-federal-government -richard-cheng-bridget-dongarra.

11. Kathryn Dill, "The Top 25 Companies that Will Let You Work from Home," https://www.cnbc.com/2017/01/31/the-top-25-companies-that -will-let-you-work-from-home.html.

12. Rita Gunther McGrath, "Failure Is a Gold Mine for India's Tata," *Harvard Business Review*, April 11, 2011.

Chapter 7

1. Personal interview, June 3, 2019.

2. To see the detailed analysis, go to the free resources on the book website, UntappedAgility.com.

3. Jeffrey M. Hiatt, *ADKAR: A Model for Change in Business, Government and Our Community* (Loveland, CO: Prosci, 2006).

4. Robert J. Anderson and William A. Adams, *Scaling Leadership* (Hoboken, NJ: Wiley, 2019).

5. Thomas Carlyle, *On Heroes, Hero-Worship, and the Heroic in History* (London: James Fraser, 1841).

6. On his website, the theory's co-creator Paul Hersey boasts over fourteen million leaders have been formally trained in the approach: https://situational.com/.

7. Robert J. House and Terence R. Mitchell, "Path-Goal Theory of Leadership," April 1975, https://apps.dtic.mil/docs/citations/ADA009513.

8. Fred E. Fielder, *A Theory of Leadership Effectiveness* (New York: McGraw-Hill Series in Management, 1967).

9. Bernard Burnes, "Kurt Lewin and the Harwood Studies: The Foundations of OD," *Journal of Applied Behavioral Science* 43, no. 2 (2007).

10. Daniel Goleman, "Leadership That Gets Results," *Harvard Business Review* (March–April 2000), https://hbr.org/2000/03/leadership-that-gets-results.

11. Robert J. Anderson and William A. Adams, *Mastering Leadership* (Hoboken, NJ: Wiley, 2016).

12. Bill Joiner and Stephen Josephs, *Leadership Agility* (San Francisco: Jossey-Bass, 2007).

13. *Finding Mastery* podcast, https://findingmastery.net/category/podcasts/.

14. "Satya Nadella, Microsoft CEO," *Finding Mastery* podcast, May 9, 2018, https://findingmastery.net/satya-nadella/.

15. Richard Branson, "What's the Health of Your Success?" Virgin, May 17, 2017, https://www.virgin.com/richard-branson/whats-health-your-success.

16. Joel Gascoigne, "My Morning Routine as a Remote CEO and Why It's Always Changing," podcast, https://open.buffer.com/morning-routine-remote-ceo/.

17. Andrew Merle, "This Is When Successful People Wake Up," *Huffington Post*, July 17, 2017, https://www.huffpost.com/entry/this-is-when-successful-people-wake-up_b_596d17a3e4b0376db8b65a1a.

18. Michael Hyatt, "Hit the Ground Writing," https://michaelhyatt.com/consistent-journaling/.

19. Catherine Clifford, "Bill Gates Took Solo 'Think Weeks' in a Cabin in the Woods—Why It's a Great Strategy," *Make It*, July 28, 2019, https://www.cnbc.com/2019/07/26/bill-gates-took-solo-think-weeks-in-a-cabin-in-the-woods.html.

20. Bill Campbell, *Trillion Dollar Coach* (New York: Alphabet, 2019).

21. Peter Bregman, "How to Ask for Feedback That Will Actually Help You," *Harvard Business Review*, December 5, 2014, https://hbr.org/2014/12/how-to-ask-for-feedback-that-will-actually-help-you.

22. Free templates are available at the book website, UntappedAgility.com.

Chapter 8

1. Jim Collins, *Good to Great* (New York: Harper Business, 2011).

2. "TEDxVictoria—Dave Morris: The Way of Improvisation," YouTube, https://youtube.com/watch?v=MUO-pWJ0riQ.

3. *Forrest Gump*, directed by R. Zemeckis (Los Angeles: Paramount Pictures, 1994).

Chapter 9

1. Forty-one percent of respondents were either actively searching for a new job or planned to start in the coming year. https://www.fastcompany.com/3065845/why-nearly-half-of-workers-globally-could-leave-their-jobs-in-2017.

Acknowledgments

I owe so much to so many. I've done a lot of writing projects in the past, but this book represents the culmination of a dream. For that, I am filled with gratitude.

To the leaders who gave me a shot at this business in the first place: Sarah Coburn, the gang at Excella (especially Jeff Galimore), Jim Cundiff, Mike Cottmeyer, Dennis Stevens, Mike Griffiths, and Tom Reinsel.

To the colleagues who have recently validated and cemented my philosophy on change: Pete Behrens, who has propelled my journey every time we've crossed paths. Luke Hohmann, a friend and a mentor who's shown me how to change the world. The PMO crew of Mark Price Perry, Andy Jordan, Michael Hannan, and Laura Barnard.

To the heroes portrayed in the book: Gretchen, Randy, Howard and Melissa, Janice, Michael, Brian, Michaela, Luis, and Randy. You are the inspiration we need to create a better workplace.

To the reviewers, who tolerated a horribly clunky first draft and lighted a path forward: Mary Bobbit, Linda Rising, Sherild Sanfilez, Apriel Biggs, and Catherine Weisser.

To the Berrett-Koehler team, who consistently defy the stereotypes and horror stories writers hear about publishing houses. Especially Charlotte Ashlock, who is the best collaborator I could have hoped for.

To the Fewell Innovation team, especially Taylor Hageman and Aaron Means, for juggling all the balls I throw at you!

To the clan: Seema, Ajay, Shanti, Akash (and Patricia). You were *the* encouraging force during the ups and downs.

Index

About the Author

J esse Fewell is an author, coach, and trainer who helps senior leaders from Boston to Beijing transform their organizations to achieve more innovation, collaboration, and business agility.

A project management pioneer, he founded and grew the original Agile Community of Practice within the Project Management Institute (PMI) to 18,000 members and 40 volunteer leaders. He also co-created the PMI-ACP® agile certification and has served on leadership subcommittees for the Scrum Alliance.

Jesse has directly taught, keynoted, or coached thousands of leaders and practitioners across thirteen countries on five continents. His insights have come from diverse sources, whether it has been coaching leaders in Global 1000 organizations like GE, Philips, and Verizon, or serving as the inaugural speaker at Scrum Bangalore and organizing the Agile Leadership Network of Washington, D.C.

Jesse's writings on management and leadership have been translated into eleven languages and reached over a half million readers. They include:

- Contributions to five international management standards, including the coauthoring of 2017's *Agile Practice Guide®* and the upcoming *Guide to the PMBOK® Guide–Seventh Edition*.
- His column *The Agile Project Manager* has appeared in multiple management publications over the last ten years.

- He distilled his global leadership experiences in the limited edition handbook *Can You Hear Me Now: Leading Global, Distributed, Virtual Teams.*

A graduate of Johns Hopkins University, Jesse is a multi-certified leadership coach (Scrum Alliance®, the Leadership Circle®) and an accredited instructor with multiple certification bodies (Scrum Alliance, SAFe, ICAgile). His industry contributions earned him a 2013 IEEE Computer Society Golden Core Award.

For more information about Jesse, go to the book website, UntappedAgility.com, where you can also download several free resources.

Dear reader,

Thank you for picking up this book and welcome to the worldwide BK community! You're joining a special group of people who have come together to create positive change in their lives, organizations, and communities.

What's BK all about?

Our mission is to connect people and ideas to create a world that works for all.

Why? Our communities, organizations, and lives get bogged down by old paradigms of self-interest, exclusion, hierarchy, and privilege. But we believe that can change. That's why we seek the leading experts on these challenges—and share their actionable ideas with you.

A welcome gift

To help you get started, we'd like to offer you a **free copy** of one of our bestselling ebooks:

www.bkconnection.com/welcome

When you claim your **free ebook**, you'll also be subscribed to our blog.

Our freshest insights

Access the best new tools and ideas for leaders at all levels on our blog at ideas.bkconnection.com.

Sincerely,

Your friends at Berrett-Koehler

Certified

Corporation